1995 EDITION

Selling Songs Successfully

By
Henry Boye

LIFETIME BOOKS, INC.
2131 Hollywood Blvd., Suite 305
Hollywood, FL 33020

Copyright © 1994 by Henry Boye

All rights reserved. Published simultaneously in Canada by Lifetime Books, Inc.

Reproduction or translation of any part of this work beyond that permitted by Section 107 or 108 of the 1976 Copyright Act without the permission of the copyright owner is unlawful. Requests for permission or further information should be addressed to the Permissions Department, Lifetime Books, Inc., 2131 Hollywood Boulevard, Hollywood, FL 33020.

This publication is designed to provide accurate and authoritative information in regard to the subject matter covered. It is sold with the understanding that the publisher is not engaged in rendering legal, accounting, or other professionall service. If legal advice or other expert assistance is required, the services of a competent professional person should be sought. *From a Declaration of Principles jointlly adopted by a Committee of the American Bar Association and a Committee of Publishers.*

Library of Congress Cataloging-in-Publication Data

Boye, Henry.
  Selling songs successfully / by Henry Boye.
   p.   cm.
  Includes index.
  ISBN 0-8119-0798-8   : $14.95
  1. Popular music-writing and publishing.   2. Sound recording industry.   I. Title.
MT67.B64 1994
782.42164′068′8-dc20   94-30255
                                                       CIP
                                                       MN

Manufactured in the United States of America
1 2 3 4 5 6 7 8 9 0

Contents

Foreword iii
1 Introduction 1
2 Enthusiasm 5
3 Hustle 9
4 Stick-to-itiveness 13
5 Success Stories 17
6 Preparing Your Song 23
7 Publicity 29
8 Beginning to Sell 33
9 Selling Points 37
10 The Letter of Introduction 41
11 Mailing Your Songs 45
12 Contacts 49
13 The A&R Men 51
14 Indie Record Producers 55
15 Meeting the Entertainers 61
16 Collaboration 65
17 Songwriter's Clubs and
     Custom Recordings 69
18 Promotion 73
19 Performance Royalties and
     Clearance Societies 81
20 Thar's Gold in Them Thar Hills 93
21 The Musical Stage Show 99
22 How to Save Money
     Copyrighting Your Songs 105
23 Avoiding the Songsharks 109
24 "Angles" and Making Deals 113
25 Important Do's and Dont's for
     Selling Songs Successfully 115
26 The Basic ABC's for
     Selling Songs Successfully 119
27 Marketplaces 121
   Index 169

FOREWORD

Songwriting is one of the few fields that offer talented newcomers a chance to get their share of fame and fortune immediately. But most important is the pride and satisfaction of hearing *your* song on records, radio, TV, movies, jukeboxes, and everywhere that music is being played and sung today. Also, imagine that once-in-a-lifetime feeling of knowing that millions of people all over the country are hearing your creation. There is nothing like it in the world—*nothing like it at all!*

Today, the record business has reached *$5 billion* in sales and is growing bigger every year. With record sales at an all-time high and music concerts at the highest box office level ever, songs dominate the entertainment business more than ever before.

There are songs being heard and played everywhere today. We hear them in diners; they are being plugged into banks, office buildings and elevators all over the country. We hear them on airplanes flying coast to coast and all over the world; they are played in doctors' and dentists' waiting rooms; and of course, songs on records are being played on radio twenty-four hours a day.

Don't forget movies and television, which are becoming more music-oriented and are featuring all types of music. This is creating an ever-increasing need for more and more new songs; and that's where you, the new songwriter, can finally get your opportunity for fame and fortune once you've learned the basics for SELLING SONGS SUCCESSFULLY!

1

INTRODUCTION

The fact that the population of the United States is soaring past the 250 million mark is not news in itself. But what makes this important to you, the songwriter, is that almost the whole population is connected with the music industry in one way or another. This includes the amateur and the professional songwriters, the music publishers, the record companies, the recording artists, the disc jockeys, the buyers and sellers of everything pertaining to music, and finally, the music-listening public.

There are probably millions of songwriters in every part of the world who feel they have written hit songs—if only they could be sold and brought before the public. Few songwriters invest their time, energy, money, and creativity without hoping to become financially successful, perhaps entering the music industry's hall of fame as a leading hit writer. However, it is one thing to write a song and something else again to *sell* one.

The real job on a song begins *after* you write it. Your song will remain nothing more than a creative endeavor unless you learn how to sell it to the music buyers. What you do, how you do it, and what happens afterwards will determine the ultimate fate of your song.

A highly concentrated, concerted, and continuous effort is required from the songwriter, who must have enough confidence in his work to go out and do something about it to begin to even hope for a hit. Anyone can write a song, be it good or bad, but statistics prove that the average person's chances of being struck by lightning are greater than his chances of coming up with a hit song. Right from the start you must learn that selling your songs is a big, hard job, especially if you know very little about the business. So be prepared to go about it in a big way.

Quick and easy shortcuts don't exist in the music field. It's a highly specialized and highly competitive business. When you visit the music centers, or drop your songs into the mail, you go into competition with every songwriter in the world. Therefore, you can't expect the record companies and recording artists to record your song unless it contains something to make them *want* to look at it or listen to it. You must make them think they will be losing out on something if they pass up your song.

Songwriters must therefore concentrate on new ways of putting their songs across—clever ways of campaigning and bringing their songs to the attention of the VIPs in the music industry. In this stiff field of competition, the songwriter's only chance for success lies in his ingenuity—his ability to devise ways to get his songs into the right places. Songwriters should be prepared to grasp every opportunity offered them, take advantage of every break given to them. The philosopher Demosthenes once said: "Small opportunities are often the beginning of great enterprises."

If you have been previously pessimistic, waiting for luck to come your way, a change in attitude will help you to take that first big step up the ladder of songwriting success. As Bernard M. Baruch once said, "When the outlook is steeped in pessimism, I remind myself, 'Two and two still makes four, and you can't keep mankind down for long.'"

The following pages cover most of the TRICKS and TACT I have learned during my many professional years in the trade as well as the TRAITS you must develop to give it your best shot. Whether you succeed or fail may depend on your learning these methods—IT'S UP TO YOU!

2

ENTHUSIASM

Enthusiasm is an inherent trait among all ambitious and creative people, and a determining factor in selling songs successfully. It is the key to personal success.

The moment you let your enthusiasm die down or entertain no more thoughts of some expected pleasure or profit; the moment you lose interest in some future opportunity—at that moment your mental machinery begins to slow down!

Enthusiasm is something you must have every day; it builds and builds and grows and grows. Enthusiasm can be the driving force that spurs you into trying harder and doing your best work. It instills confidence in your work and you. It's contagious—a quality that may be instrumental in making your contacts believe in you and your efforts.

Surely you wrote your songs with enthusiasm, and you should be able to carry that enthusiasm into your job of selling. Enthusiasm can bring you into a music publisher's or record company's office with the feeling that perhaps today is the day. It can give you a cheerful outlook that makes you feel and look good. It lets you see yourself happy, confident, and succeeding in your venture.

Enthusiasm as the effect of life's hands lifting you with eagerness and excitement, making you ready to accept the challenges you will face when you try to sell your songs. Or thing of it this way—enthusiasm can be the catalyst that launches you to the start of a new career; it can be the starting point of a hit song, the match that lights the creative fire in you. Throw yourself into your worthwhile goal. Lose yourself in it, and results will surely follow.

Get excited about your songwriting. Take time to appreciate the wonder of it all. Enjoying what you are doing will make reaching your goal easier. Activity you would rather not be doing is work, but work you do with enthusiasm is pleasure. It gives you that positive outlook on life that says you *can* and *will* reach exciting new heights of achievement and realize great personal rewards.

A wise man once said: "No one keeps up his enthusiasm automatically. Enthusiasm must be nourished with new actions, new aspirations, new efforts, new vision. It is one's own fault if his enthusiasm is gone. He has failed to feed it!"

Enthusiasm can also turn your talent, whether it is writing lyrics, poetry, verse or music, into an enjoyable and possibly profitable hobby. Everyone should have a hobby as a sideline for their creativity, and if it expands into bigger things, all the better. Songwriting can become not only a game and a challenge, but a rewarding hobby as well.

The bigger the challenge, the more valued the rewards. Enthusiasm offers you a chance at that reward. So whether songwriting brings you your well-deserved fame and fortune or becomes only an enjoyable hobby, it can be your stepping stone to the VIPs in the music industry.

3
HUSTLE

Later on in the book, I will elaborate further on these two methods; but for now, I have outlined the first and most important step toward selling your songs successfully: HUSTLE—*creative* and *physical!*

I will add two key words to differentiate between the two types of hustle that are available to all of us. One I call "*creative* hustle," which can be defined as the ability to think, plan, and mail your songs while sitting in the comfort of your home. The other is "*physical* hustle," which is the ability to run, visit, and seek out personally those people in the music industry who can help you most with your songs. Abraham Lincoln said it better than I: "Things may come to those who wait—but only the things left by those who hustle!"

Creative hustle means being always alert for any and all leads that help you sell your songs. Newsstands carry most of the important trade magazines covering the music field. To keep abreast of the music business, it is imperative that you read and absorb at least one, if not all, of these magazines. Some of the well-known ones that should be available to you are *Billboard, Cashbox,* and *Variety.* They will tell you who and where the new and active artists are and where they are appearing. Informative columns and features will also point out who the new and rising music executives are and where you will be able to reach them.

If you decide to write to these people first, don't be modest in telling them about yourself and your new songs. Politely ask them if they would be interested in helping you further your career and if you may send them some of your songs for consideration.

This letter should be as informative as you can possibly make it. Was your song performed anywhere, locally or elsewhere? On TV? On radio? In benefits or clubs? Was it used by any bands or singers? Do you have any favorable comments from others about your song? If so, put all these things into your letter. Make it a letter with a sales punch! You want to excite their curiosity enough to make them want to hear your song. Ingenuity and sincerity are all-important here. This is what is meant by creative hustle. If you have recorded your song and it has been played on disc jockey programs or even sold in record stores, don't keep it a secret. Tell everyone in the trade about it! Get a letter from the disc jockey and from the music stores that stock your record. Contact record distributors in your area so you can get wider distribution for your record and even get it placed in local jukeboxes. Publishers want to hear that your song has been sold and heard locally. They want to feel they are considering a product that has been commercially accepted in your area. Then they may be willing to buy it, or get a major record firm to take it over, and then put money behind it for fully national distribution and airplay. If you are really a go-getter, a physical hustler, patronize the places where entertainers are appearing and get to meet them personally. Then take advantage of such meetings by asserting your salesmanship and enthusiasm.

You must try to interest them in giving your songs a chance to be heard. Don't be overforceful or rude by show your enthusiasm, being courteous and tactful at all times. Remember, these entertainers have achieved some status in the music field; you need them more than they need you at this time. Being there in person also gives you the advantage of being able to sway their "no's" to "yeses." If the entertainer agrees to listen to your song, you will at least feel the evening's expenses were worthwhile. This form of selling is what is meant by *physical hustle*.

This is the method I prefer to use, because the physical hustle approach is personal. It gives you instant contact with the artist and possibly his manager. You can write them about your new songs in the future, knowing they are familiar with you and therefore may be more than willing to give you a hearing. Personal contact—personal hustle—does pay off.

4

STICK-TO-ITIVENESS

The next important trait you must adapt to, and a worthy follow-up to hustle, is "stick-to-itiveness." Unless it becomes an important part of your hustle, neither one of these traits will help you find success.

Stick-to-itiveness is a combination of two concepts: *stick to it* and initiative.

Initiative means that you must get up, get out, and hustle. You must take it upon yourself to make the first moves and approaches. Take the initiative. Be a leader. Set an example for others to follow. It is up to you to grasp at any and every opportunity open to you or to make these opportunities open up for you. Then, after taking the initiative, say to yourself, "I know I can do it. I will do it. I will succeed," and *stick to it!*

Most people do accept challenges and the opportunities offered by such challenges. Focus and build on human potentials—yours and others. Keep an UP attitude about yourself and your songwriting efforts. Stick-to-itiveness is what the life preserver is to the nonswimmer. You must have it with you at all times or you will surely go under.

Perseverance prevails! If you remember these key words, you will have another meaning for stick-to-itiveness. Using it will help you towards selling your songs successfully. If you persevere, you will prevail and prosper.

Many people who develop the hustle so necessary in this business lose out because they are easily discouraged by failures, lack of responses, and the seemingly long time it takes them to place their songs. You must learn to take the bad with the good. Keep on smiling and trying. A smile is contagious, and whatever good goes from you will eventually come back to you. Share the sunshine and keep on plugging away. Keep your enthusiasm going and *stick to it!*

It is the rare songwriter indeed who has immediate success in placing his songs. You need time to learn to take the initiative, stick to it, and hustle, never giving in to disappointment and discouragement, until you finally make the grade. If you are prepared to work hard at this, you will be selling songs successfully in the near future. There are no shortcuts, but this book should make your wait much shorter by showing the shortest, most successful path.

Stick-to-itiveness is a great element of success. If you only knock long enough and loud enough at the door, you are sure to wake up somebody. Don't just sit back and take what comes; go after what you want. Anybody can give up. The thing to do is *keep* up.

If you are now further prepared to work hard and to put your wholehearted effort behind your songs, you will find that eventually your hustle and stick-to-itiveness will start paying dividends in responses, encouragements, acceptances, and finally, the exalted feeling of a job well done when you hear *your* song on the air for the first time.

To summarize; if you were to add up any column of song hits, it would balance out to read: ENTHUSIASM PLUS HUSTLE PLUS STICK-TO-ITIVENESS EQUALS SUCCESS!

5

SUCCESS STORIES

To inspire, encourage, and show you that it can be done and is being done every day, let me relate some success stories of people who did reach fame and fortune in the music industry after learning how to sell songs successfully. Each started out to be a songwriter and all showed the qualities common to success—enthusiasm, hustle, and stick-to-itiveness.

Our first success story began in Detroit, where Berry Gordy Jr. was holding down a steady job in an automobile factory while dreaming that his songs would some day bring him riches. When he finally wrote a song he was enthused with and believed in, he borrowed seven hundred dollars—a lot of money in those days—to record his tune "Way Over There" with a vocal group called The Miracles. It was an appropriate name for them and for Berry Gordy Jr., because although the song wasn't the hit they had hoped for, their faith and stick-to-itiveness compelled them to continue trying and they were rewarded with hit after hit.

Six short years later, the ex-auto worker was not only a millionaire songwriter, but owner and president of Tamla Motown Record Corporation, one of the industry's most successful combines, encompassing a top music publishing company, a profitable talent management agency, and one of the largest independent record companies functioning anywhere. In fact, not forgetting that all this came from humble beginnings in the automobile-building city, Berry Gordy Jr. named his operation MOTOWN, which stands for Motor Town—Detroit, Michigan

Berry Gordy Jr. became one of the richest black men in the country—a multimillionaire many times over. He sold his record and music firm to one of the biggest music conglomerates in the world for several hundred million dollars.

The Miracles not only went on to become one of the all-time biggest selling groups in the Rhythm and Blues field, but their leader, Smokey Robinson, became vice-president of the company. He also continues writing songs, singing, and producing records for the firm.

One young Canadian songwriter started out in Ottawa, Canada. He was a child prodigy who always liked to write and sing songs, so it wasn't long before he put all his talents to good use.

At the age of fifteen, he had a crush on a girl who was a bit older than he. Her name, put into song by this aspiring songwriter/singer, would be spoken over record-sales counters nine *million times.* "Diana" became one of the first large-selling singles in the history of the record business.

Fame and fortune came quickly to this bright new talent, and "Diana" was soon followed by a pair of other million-sellers: "Put Your Head On My Shoulder" and "You Are My Destiny." From there, he went on to write "Puppy Love," "She's A Lady," "My Way," and the theme song for Johnny Carson's *Tonight Show;* appropriately titled "Johnny's Theme."

Paul Anka was also enormously skillful at writing songs geared to the talents of other artists. His lyrics for one song perfectly summed up what was identified as the essence of Frank Sinatra's life. It is the enormously successful "My Way. 11

When he wrote "She's A Lady" for Tom Jones, many thought it was a positive statement by Tom about his lovely wife, a feeling that Paul Anka aimed at and tried to convey when he wrote it.

Anka has written and performed songs that have earned him at least twenty gold records, making him one of the biggest selling singers and top songwriters in the music industry. When he sold his Spanka Music Publishing Company for a top seven-figure sum, he became a millionaire many times over.

In 1970, with no money to speak of, a young aspiring songwriter/singer came to Nashville convinced he would make it to the top in no time at all. Unfortunately, without the know-how or any contacts to turn to, he found his early career in dire trouble. He began knocking on the doors of record companies and spent most of those years sleeping in his car or in cheap slum hotels.

"I thought I knew everything when I came to Nashville, but now I'm sure I wasn't ready," he stated. He kept working on his songs and finally prevailed upon a very small record company called "Crazy Mama" to let him sing and record his own compositions. Although it came from an unknown songwriter and artist, one of his songs made some noise around the music trade and it was brought to the attention of Larry Butler, record producer for the top Country and Western recording artist, Kenny Rogers.

The song destined to bring fortune and fame to songwriter Don Schlitz was the big hit "The Gambler." Don had kept "The Gambler" on the shelf for *two years* after writing it because he didn't think too much of it. He had only spent twenty minutes writing it, and he had put it aside to work on several other song ideas he wanted to develop.

Don Schlitz passes on these important words to all aspiring songwriters: "You can sit home and write songs, but that doesn't make a recording; it doesn't get the song out; and it doesn't put a record on the market. I try to write a lot of songs to share with people. You share it by going out and doing the legwork. And you definitely don't do it by yourself. If you think you do, you're going to be disappointed. I try to write a song so that the person who is listening to it will say, 'Hey, man, he wrote that song about me', or 'That song fits me.'"

"The Gambler" went on to win the Grammy Award, and thanks to the royalties, Don Schlitz was able to attend the ceremonies in the first real suit of clothes he ever owned.

In his acceptance speech, Don said the things I wish for all of you trying to write that hit song: "I'm having the time of my life and it's not going to stop, because I'm working very hard and love what I'm doing!"

Hopefully, the success stories have your adrenalin flowing and you are ready to try for that elusive songwriting career. So read on, because you are about to enter the fascinating and exciting field of SELLING SONGS SUCCESSFULLY!

6

PREPARING YOUR SONG

You now have the enthusiasm; you're prepared to hustle; you're determined to stick to it; now you're ready to enter the first basic phase of the songwriting business. And songwriting is a very big business.

The basis of the music business is the song; and the most creative person in the entire industry is the songwriter. But merely creating a song is only the beginning. Preparing and selling it are the tasks that make a creative product a reality.

Before you can even think about entering this fascinating and highly rewarding industry, you need to develop the necessary tools. The first step is to have copies of your songs printed. This could be a simple, inexpensive *lead-sheet* or a professional copy made up for you by a musical arranger. A lead-sheet is simply a copy of musical notes depicting the melody, with typed or handwritten lyrics beneath the notes. A "professional" copy is one printed for commercial use which shows musical notes, chords, and progressions for various instruments, and professionally printed lyrics.

Many songwriters, including some of the bigger names in the songwriting field, can't read or write music. I'm also included in this group, but this is not a big handicap. There are professional helpers on call in the music field, known as musical stenographers, who will gladly transpose your song onto paper for a small fee.

This is how it works: You can either sing your song to them in person or have a simple, inexpensive voice recording made for them. After getting a fair idea of your melody, they will then pick out the notes on their piano and transpose them onto sheets of staff-lined, musical manuscript paper. This will be a satisfactory lead-sheet of your song ready for the music trade to evaluate.

There are many of these arrangers and musical stenographers listed in your classified telephone directory under the heading "Music Arrangers." Of course, you may have friends adept at the piano or other musical instruments who wouldn't mind preparing the lead-sheet to help you out. A lead-sheet is also necessary for registering your song for copyright. Once you've established yourself in the trade, you can start submitting your songs with demos and sheets of paper containing lyrics only. The music publisher will take care of the lead-sheet.

Once you have a professional-looking lead-sheet with the correct notes and lyrics printed on it, it is time to start selling. But when you start showing it around, you may find that there is no interest, and it is returned to you after one quick glance. Why? Often because you neglected to choose a *saleable title* that intrigues the buyers so they will want to read or listen further.

To write a commercial song you must first select a commercial title—a title that will appeal to the public's taste. After all, the public will ultimately be the ones to put their money down to buy your song. So choose a title that is catchy, that has one major selling point, and *attracts attention!*

A song title can either make or break your song before you start to sell it. It's like a newspaper headline. If it doesn't attract the buyer's attention and make him want to read further, he won't buy the paper (your song).

To pick a title and song theme with public appeal, listen to the lyrics and titles of the leading songs being played today. See what they have to say and what their writers did to make them more marketable. Absorb all the ideas you possibly can. The more you learn and retain, the more you will be able to improve your own songwriting.

Once you have your properly titled lead-sheet, the next step is to have a demonstration record, known in the trade as a 'demo', made of your song. This is a *must* in selling, your songs successfully. Just as many writers can't read music, the same is true of most music publishers and recording artists; but they all do have record players.

Most recording studies in your area are equipped to produce demos. It need not be a costly recording with full chorus and orchestra. A simple demonstration record of a piano or guitar and voice rendition of your song usually is sufficient. But the more professional the presentation of your product, the more response it will receive.

Your ultimate aim, of course, is to get your song recorded commercially. The music business today revolves around the record industry. Any efforts made to sell your song successfully must therefore be aimed in the direction of record companies and recording artists. These subjects will be emphasized in later chapters.

SAMPLE PROFESSIONAL LEAD-SHEET COPY

7

PUBLICITY

Just as a title draws attention to your song, *publicity* advertises you and your product. Publicity is the basis for many songs receiving their start, and new songwriters should publicize themselves and their songs whenever and wherever possible. Through publicity, you and your song efforts will be brought to the public's attention and to the attention of those people who are in a position to help you.

There are ways of getting free publicity if you know how to go about it. One good way to start is to arouse the interest of your hometown newspapers. If you can convince them that there is a lot of human interest in your story, they may be willing to publish an item about the rising talents of a local son or daughter. There are always a few kind editors around who are willing to give struggling fledglings a helping hand to further their careers. Your local editor is always open to suggestions and stories with local color. Why not try talking to him?

If you can't get to see the editors or don't wish to visit them, here's another approach. Print up copies of resumés except, instead of calling them resumés use the words "NEWS RELEASE" in bold letters as the headline. Include a good picture of yourself, possibly holding one or more of your songs, and include your name, address, and telephone number. Then write a little story about yourself, what you are doing now and what you hope to do in the songwriting field. Add any successes you may have had and anything else that may add local color and interest.

Send these out to the editors of your community newspapers and even to the larger metropolitan papers in your city. Editors are always looking for interesting hometown news to fill open spaces. You will be doing their staff a favor by saving them time searching for these fillers, and you may reap publicity rewards at the same time.

You can also use these "news releases" as appealing flyers and fact sheets for those people who are most interested in your songwriting career—bands, performers, and recording studios.

You can also place spot ads about your songs in various music or trade publications, or anywhere else the entertainment world may read them. Don't go to the extremes of expensive ads in the hope they will launch your songwriting career unless you have the extra money to spare. Great benefits can be gained by small, inexpensive ads if you can come up with a novel eye-opener to attract attention.

Your library is an excellent place to find Reference Guides which will list media contacts for you to write to for ad rates! For names and addresses, refer to these resources:

Bacon's Publicity Checker (Directory of newspapers and magazines); Editor and Publisher Yearbook (directory of newspapers with names of section editors); Gale Directory of Publications (newspapers and magazines); Standard Periodical Directory (directory of magazines).

If you were able to come up with a commercial recording of your song (whether you paid to have it made yourself, or a small record firm liked your song enough to put it on a recording), bring it to your local radio station and try to get a personal interview on the air by convincing the disc jockey or station manager of the audience interest in the local-boy approach. It will help if you tell them that lots of your friends, neighbors, and relatives will also be tuned in to their station. You should try to PUBLICIZE and PROMOTE your songs in any *and every* way possible.

Publicity should be a regular part of your planning. Well thought-out publicity can help launch your songwriting career. Be creative. Learn all you can about publicity procedures by reading about it, and always be persistent in trying to attract the VIPs attention.

The songwriter who waits for the world to beat a path to his door is a great optimist. But put a "welcome mat" out and people will know where you live. That is publicity. Doing without publicity is like the man winking at a pretty girl in the dark-the man knows what he's doing but nobody else does!

Talk it up! Spreading the word around about your songwriting ambitions just might get the message to the right ears. If you don't tell people about your talents, no one else will.

8

BEGINNING TO SELL

A songwriter must learn to become a businessman—a clever businessman who will handle himself successfully and make the cash registers keep on ringing up the sales. Your songs are a commodity that you will be placing on the selling market.

Perhaps you have never sold anything, but the records show that people in all walks of life—truck drivers and gas station attendants, teachers and students, clerks and housewives—have proved that it is possible to master the techniques of SELLING SONGS SUCCESSFULLY!

You will have to act like a salesman, because no one else will sell your product for you. You are the one who believes in your products, and your job is to create a situation where other people will feel they will be losing a good thing if they don't buy your song. You must continue to talk it up, build it up, and show it off so others will also start believing in it.

You have to feel that you have exactly what the public wants before you can begin to sell your song. You want the public to get to know your product and accept it. To do this you have to start with your creative talent and create what others will run out to buy.

You must grasp at any and all opportunities because you never know when another opportunity may present itself. You must also become an *opportunist.* This means you must make opportunities open up for you.

That contrary music publisher isn't going to come knocking at your door. Neither will that busy A&R man; and certainly don't expect a visit from the much-traveled and besieged entertainer. Nobody in the music industry even knows that you exist. So you have to change all that!

Songwriters should try to please as many people as possible. While you should write what you write best, you should keep the buying public in mind. Unless the public is playing, using, and buying your songs, you cannot be considered a success. Keep the public in mind and try to develop that uncanny sense of what everyone might want.

Let us begin with the songs you have written that you feel are ready for market. Take one of them out and study it. Think! Did you write it with any particular artist in mind? Did you write it in the vein of a song that became a hit? N"at record company releases this type of song successfully? When you have thought about these questions, put your answers down on a list and look it over. What you have come up with, whether you realize it or not, is a plan of operation.

Every week you should write or visit at least three of the important contacts you should have put on a list. By making **it** a point to follow through on this, you will be presented with opportunities by receiving an answer or two. Keep at it until you connect.

The more people you get to meet in the music industry, the better your chances are of linking up with the right one. This selling method will also help you get to know who is buying songs at the present time. Being in the right place at the right time is as good a formula for selling songs successfully as it is for any other endeavor you undertake. Trips to the music centers to meet and mingle with others and discuss selling tips with them are also helpful. Their tips can steer you to valuable leads. Follow each and every one of them. Their path may lead to your success.

9

SELLING POINTS

Other selling points can further enhance your chances. You must surround yourself with an aura of originality and ingenuity.

Naturally, I can't begin to tell you how to be original or clever; but I will try to stimulate your thoughts and inspire your mind by showing you how other songwriters, including myself, used their natural attributes effectively. Years ago, a young, ambitious songwriter had written a song he felt was suitable for top singer Perry Como. He tried constantly to see Como personally but he always found him "not in" or too busy to see anyone. He then sent his song, unsolicited, to Perry Como's office. Of course, his material was returned unopened and marked "refused."

Finally, risking his college savings and other borrowed money, he ordered an advertisement billboard similar to those you may have seen hanging from some of the larger buildings overlooking Times Square in New York City. On it, in big, bold letters he had a message printed that read something like this:

DEAR PERRY COMO:
 I HAVE WRITTEN A SONG FOR YOU TO SING. PLEASE GIVE ME A CHANCE AND LISTEN TO IT!

(SONGWRITER'S NAME)
(ADDRESS)
(PHONE NUMBER)

Perry Como invited the enterprising songwriter to bring the song to his office, and the publicity in trade journals and other media earned him more calls and letters from interested music publishers, artists, and record companies asking him to submit his songs to them also.

Other songwriters have called at publishers' offices pretending to be messengers of singing telegrams. Once admitted, they proceeded to sing their new songs to surprised officers. Still others have cornered music executives in elevators, and by the time the execs had reached their floors, the songwriters had glibly persuaded them to take their songs for evaluation.

One clever songwriter spotted a music publisher dining in his usual music center restaurant. When the publisher finished his meal and called for his check, instead of presenting the check, the waiter handed the astonished publisher a note left in its place by the enterprising songwriter. The note read:

Dear Sir:

I have taken the liberty of paying your luncheon check, which I calculated would have amounted to my probable expenses for coming into New York and making phone calls trying to see you.

In return, I anticipate your permission to allow this talented songwriter an interview to play some of his material for your possible acceptance.

(SONGWRITER'S NAME)
(ADDRESS)
(PHONE NUMBER)

I may not have been as ingenious as these songwriters when I started out, but I did come up with a clever gimmick to publicize myself and my songs. I appeared in front of buildings where music publishers and record companies were located, wearing a T-shirt on which was printed in big, bold letters:

TOP SONGWRITER—HIT SONGS

**HENRY BOYE
(PHONE NUMBER)**

I was approached by many vocal and instrumental groups looking for new songs to help them get started. Two small music publishers, who also owned their own record companies, stopped to talk to me. They not only helped launch my songwriting career, but they also became my best friends and they have remained so for the past twenty-five years.

These are just a few of the many gimmicks that have helped me and other songwriters sell successfully. Hopefully they will inspire you to think up some of your own or rework these to put to use for yourself.

10

THE LETTER OF INTRODUCTION

I have explained briefly the importance of publicizing your talent and I have told you about some clever selling ideas used by other songwriters to draw attention to their talents. There is also a very important, though less dramatic, method of introduction to the people in the music industry.

As documented in the previous chapter, the songwriter who sends his song to a well-known artist, publisher, and producers will invariably have it returned unopened and marked "REFUSED." A basic rule in selling songs successfully is to *never* mail your songs unsolicited to any VIP. Always ask for permission first.

The following sample letter of introduction has been used successfully by the author. It has frequently brought quick replies to send my songs for consideration and possible use. Naturally, you should not copy this letter word for word. But you can follow it as a guide and outline.

SAMPLE LETTER OF INTRODUCTION

Mr. or Ms.. Entertainer
c/o Record Company
Address, City & State

Dear (name of entertainer):

I am looking for an artist in your position who would be kind and interested enough to help me expand my career as a songwriter. As a top performer, you are no doubt always looking for new material to further your career.

I am writing you because your style is suited to a particular song I have written, and I feel we may be able to get together for a successful association. I write mainly ballads, and one I would like you to consider is entitled "One Life, One Love, One You." It has been featured by a local band at weddings and has been received enthusiastically.

I would greatly appreciate your taking a moment to check the box on the self-addressed postal card. Thank you for your time and I eagerly await your reply. Either way you may decide, I wish you good luck and continued success.

Sincerely yours,

(SONGWRITER'S NAME)

SAMPLE OF POSTAL CARD ENCLOSED
Please send songs for consideration.
Tape ☐ Cassette ☐ Lead-sheet ☐
Sorry, I can't help you at this time ☐
Try me again, later ☐
REMARKS:

_____
_____
_____
_____

_____ SIGNATURE

Don't forget to put your return name and address on the other side of the postal card. As I told you earlier, originality is a strong selling point; so if you can improve on these samples by using new or better words and tricks of your own, do so!

Remember that you have to *sell yourself* in your letter of introduction, so express your own personality as much as possible.

11

MAILING YOUR SONGS

Once you have received an answer to your letter of introduction granting you permission to send your songs, you must get on with the "creative hustle" method of selling songs successfully. But a word of warning, concentrate on your *best* songs. Don't just throw any of your songs indiscriminately into the mail, thinking you're better off with more "irons in the fire." The coals will prove to be "ice-cold." And don't think your song is good just because a friend or relative was kind enough to tell you so. Try to get your friends to buy a copy of your song if you want to know what they really think of it.

Always be dissatisfied with your work and continually try to improve it. A good trick for testing the strength of your song is to put it aside after completion and not go near it for a day or two. When you do return to it, if you can still feel the same enthusiasm for it that you did before, you might have a good song to work with.

There is still no guarantee that the record companies or artists will look at your songs once they are mailed in. These people are absorbed with a hundred other things, so you must be prepared to be ignored. In most cases, it is also an expensive proposition, because your demo records may not be returned despite the fact that you enclosed postage for their safe return. I always send a recording tape or cassette on which I transferred at least three of my songs from the original demonstration records. In that way I eliminate the cost of postage for several demos. Cassettes and tapes are also easier to package and handle. Every record company and artist has a tape recorder or cassette player. The cost of a cassette is negligible compared to the cost of making duplicate two-sided acetate demos. Either way, mailing in your material is a necessary expense in today's competitive market.

Once you get permission, don't waste your song copies needlessly. Recording companies and their roster of artists specialize in certain types of songs. One performer doesn't sing rock and roll; another may prefer only ballads; a third may sing country and western exclusively. The same situation exists at record companies where one A&R director may go for one type of tune and another finds his hits with a different style of music. Therefore, study the markets you intend to reach; if your song is suited for one particular artist or record company, concentrate on mailing to them first. The easiest way to get your break and possibly get your song recorded is to slant your material to fit the exact style of a hot-selling recording artist.

When you have decided upon the people you will try to reach, I suggest you reach them all. The more people you can find who will consider your songs, the better your chances of selling them.

To further improve my chances over competitors, I have discovered through trial and error the *key time* for mailing out songs. Most people are more attuned to their work on specific days of the week. During and just before the weekends, your VIPs will have their minds on recreational outlets, socializing, or just relaxing from their work schedule. Therefore, it stands to reason that sending out songs to reach them on or near the weekends will not get your songs the objective hearing you wish.

Also try to eliminate Mondays. Their desks are usually piled high with work that was left from Friday and received on Saturday. VIPs will not have time to give your songs the close attention you would like. They will go through an "automatic" routine, with their thoughts on other Monday schedules. You should, therefore, arrange to have your songs reach your chosen destination on *Tuesday, Wednesday, or Thursday.*

Just as there are key *days*, there are also good and bad *months* to send your songs. The first two months of the year, January and February, and the fall months of September and October are usually the best months for mailing to the VIPs. During these months, they are apt to be more active in mind and body and better able to concentrate on their jobs.

The worst months are the summer months, because that is vacation time; and most will be on, or at least anticipating, their long-awaited vacations. Of course, don't bother to send anything during December, since the VIPs will be more concerned with the gifts and goodies to and from others who have helped make it a successful year.

12
CONTACTS

Your letter of introduction and getting your songs into the mail will lead you to a valuable aid in selling your songs successfully—contacts.

Contacts are the people you will meet, get to know, and later turn to for help in furthering your career. They can open many doors that were previously closed to you.

You can begin where you live. Are there any recording companies nearby? Do you have any friends who work there who might introduce you to people in authority? And contacting local talent can help you gain extra promotion, exploitation, and publicity. In other words, by all means approach the big artists in the music industry; but at the same time, concentrate on the new, unknown or up-and-coming entertainers who may be right around the corner from you. They will agree to help you more often than you might think because they are basically in the same position as you: they also have unknown talent to sell!

These local entertainers can be found at parties, clubs, or almost any other function where music is featured. Always carry copies of your songs with you so that they are readily available when you run into an entertainer in a position to help you. Any local band or singer can start your song rolling. Many songs were brought to the attention of the proper people in just this way.

And many small talents grew big from single songs that became synonymous with their names. If you think about it, one song has often thrust an unknown artist into the spotlight and earned a fortune for both the artist and the songwriter. The hit song "Cry" was written by Churchill Kolman, a night watchman in a factory; and it brought quick fame to a handicapped singer—Johnny Ray—who also wrote hit songs after that. "The Happiest Girl in the Whole U.S.A." was written by a California school marm who changed her name Yvonne Vaughn to Donna Fargo. The song not only hit the top of the C&W charts, but also reached the "Top 10" on the pop charts.

So ask any and all entertainers you meet to look your song over and let you know what they think. If they like it, they may feature it in their shows. Perhaps at one of these performances, someone in the audience connected with the music business will hear it and also like it. If they are interested in the song, they will come looking for you; or if it's the band they like, the may bring the group into a studio and record them featuring *your* song. It has happened this way many times before and it could happen to you.

13

THE A&R MEN

The A&R department is the ear of any record company. When a demo tape arrives, the A&R man listens to it and evaluates it. If he and his staff like it, the song is recorded.

A&R literally means "ARTIST AND REPERTOIRE." The A&R man deals with the artist himself, the songs, and the instrumental material—the repertoire. Therefore, the A&R man holds one of the most important jobs in a record company. His job is to match the right songs with the right artists. Too many misses and he's out looking for another job. This makes him very choosy. His job hinges on picking the hits. He doesn't care who writes them or where they come from, so he is your best contact at the record companies.

Once, while I was waiting to see an A&R man at a major record company, a young man who looked about seventeen years old, came into the office and walked over to the receptionist with a large manila envelope clutched in his hands. He then told her matter-of-factly, "I'd like to see the president."

Naturally the receptionist was taken aback, but quickly regaining her composure, she asked him the same question she probably asked a hundred times a day: "Do you have an appointment?"

When the young man answered "No," she continued patiently, "What is it in reference to?"

"Oh," beamed the boy, "I wrote a song and I'd like to play it for him."

You certainly have to admire this fledgling songwriter's nerve and fortitude, but I wouldn't recommend his approach. You should try to find out the A&R man's name first. They are the only ones you should ask to see, unless you are related to, or personally know, the president of the record company. These A&R men are as important as or even more important than the president of the firm to you, the songwriter, because in most cases, *they* make the final decisions on which songs are to be recorded.

A young A&R man of a major record company stated in an interview, "You call up a record company, ask for the A&R division, and say to who answers the phone, 'I have a tape of some excellent songs.' Then you give as much information as will be helpful: the songs are in this style, the songs have been played by various groups in your area, etc. You ask if you can send the tape in for listening. You write your name, address, and phone number on the tape as well as the accompanying letter asking for a response. Say you will pick it up in a week or so, or enclose return postage for their convenience in sending your material back."

If you are lucky enough to receive a personal appointment, make valuable use of your demo. Always bring a leadsheet along so they can follow the lyrics by reading them as the record is being played—just in case the vocalist on your recording doesn't produce your words too clearly.

Don't hesitate to approach the smaller record companies. They are often more receptive to the beginning songwriter and his new songs, and they also come up with a big share of the hits. The A&R man at a smaller company can compete with the bigger, established firms only by using new songs and new, outstanding talent. The small record companies must often sell their records strictly on the basis of the song because the name artists who normally sell well are signed to the major labels.

It is important to note that the song itself is still the determining factor in selling songs successfully. An unknown, enterprising songwriter therefore, has as much of a chance of getting his song recorded as does the professional. An A&R man isn't interested in *who* wrote the song. He is only interested in whether the song itself can become a hit. When you go into a store to buy a record you heard on the radio, do you ask who wrote the song? Of course not! You are buying the song. The people you contact in the song-buying business buy for the same reason.

If you want to begin to sell your songs successfully, you must decide to give the A&R men exactly the type of songs they use. They should contain the right catchy words with the right catchy melody. A catchy title and a catchy beat can easily make you a winner. A good A&R man will listen to your song with a particular artist in mind. He is in the business to fit his artists to the songs he hears and likes. He is out to sell records and make lots of money for his record company. Unless he definitely feels his artists can make your song a hit, he will turn it down.

Remember that the artist and repertoire man is your inside contact to the stars you may not be able to reach. An okay by him will mean a definite recording for your song. Visit him if at all possible, or write to him if you aren't able to make this important personal contact. But either way, nurture him, because eventually the A&R man will be a most important link to your selling songs successfully.

14

INDIE RECORD PRODUCERS

If nobody in the record business is discovering your songs or your local talents, you may want to produce your own recording. Tell your interested group that you will bear the expense of a recording session if they will go into a recording studio to play and sing your songs. Perhaps you can even persuade them to share the expenses by telling them that you will all be working together to promote your individual talents, they as a performing group and you as a songwriter. Most groups will jump at this opportunity. I know, because my first successful recording artists, "The Emotions," were discovered in just this way. CAUTION! Unless you know what is involved in such a recording session, *don't* go into this project by yourself This intricate process is usually reserved for the artists and repertoire men of the various record companies, or the newer breed of recording men like myself—the Independent Record Producers (INDIE)—who has spent many years learning the intricacies of recording. It is also an expensive endeavor, and unless you are prepared to take the gamble and possibly lose your money, I advise you to avoid this venture.

But, if on your own you do come up with a finished recording, known in the trade as a *master recording,* you may be able to recover your expenses, or even make a profit, by getting a record company to give it wider distribution. Record companies are always in the market for master recordings. If they use yours, you and the group who performed your song will be in the running for the "gold ring." And even if you don't come up with a master-quality record after your session, you still widl have a full, vocal-orchestral *demo* record to use to showcase your songs.

If you are hesitant about risking such a project on your own, try to locate an Indic Record Producer. Their business is finding new songs and talent to record at their expense, and you may be able to interest them in your songs.

An Indic Record Producer is much like the A&R man in that they both produce a finished recording. Also, they match the right artist with the right song. The difference is that the A&R man produces records for his record label, while the Indic Record Producer can take his record to the record label that offers him the best deal.

Most A&R men must record the various artists signed to their company. They don't go out to discover new songs and artists. In this capacity, the Indic steps in and flourishes.

Record companies found they needed new songs, new talent, new sounds—an overall newness in their recordings—so they turned to this breed of A&R men who are constantly making the music industry look up and take notice. Record companies felt their A&R men would serve their purposes better if they remained "inside" the firm to record the artists signed to their labels, so they turned to the "outside" man. This "outside" man was able to get around and search out the new songs and the new artists and bring them together into a recording studio.

Many of the Indies also write their own songs and publish them along with their artists' tunes. In a way, you can't blame them for taking the play away from the music publishers—who have now become the third wheel in the selling-songs game. After all, the music publishers hesitated to take in new songs by new writers, but the Indie Record Producers didn't. The music publishers needed to find someone to record their material, so the Indie Record Producer also became a music publisher and didn't hesitate to throw his doors wide open for the new, unknown songwriter. One of the first triple-threat Indie Record Producers was a young man named Bob Crewe. He was a songwriter who gave up a profitable modeling career to become a vocalist for various record companies. Although his recording career as a vocalist didn't prove as successful as he had hoped, he studied and learned all he could about the recording end of the music business, which he put to good use in the Indie recordproducing field.

His first hit was with a group he formed from several other vocal groups. "The Four Seasons" went on from their first bit hit "Sherry" to record other tunes written by Bob Crewe and consistently hit the million seller mark. Crew went on to record many top artists whose hits he continued to write and publish. His production and publishing outfit was suitable named "Genius Incorporated."

Another unknown who hit it big came from England and worked in a most unorthodox style, which nevertheless brought him his share of fame and success as an Indie Record Producer. Andy Oldham got his start with "The Rolling Stones." He recorded them in various studios in a search to find something different. His method for capturing their new mood and sound was to rarely rehearse before a recording session but to rehearse the session as the recording was being made.

Accustomed to working in the comfortable, smaller recording studios in England, he felt uncomfortable when RCA Victor hired him and brought him to Hollywood to record. He found himself in a spacious studio and was immediately terrified by its size. He ordered all the lights put out except for one light to serve as a spotlight on the group ganged around the microphone in a corner of the studio. Even the control room was in subdued darkness. In this way, he was able once again to capture a feeling, a mood, and a *hit*.

The Indie Record Producer offers one of the best opportunities to new songwriters today and in the coming years, unless there is a drastic change in the music business.

When an Indie Record Producer is consistently successful, record companies will often attempt to secure his exclusive services. To do this, they are often prepared to offer him an important role in the firm. The Indie Record Producer is encouraged to start his own record label with the guidance and money of the major label behind him. All new songs and artists are released on this newly established label. This means more openings for the new songwriter because the creation and development of material will have to come from various sources, and one of these sources can be *you!*

To prepare you a little bit further in selling your songs to the Indie Record Producer, there are two important things of which you need to be aware. First, the Indie Producer is usually young with young ideas. Second, he is always taking the pulse of the great youth market out there. Therefore, he will need new songs with the *young* sound to fulfill his recording commitments. These young neophytes have even managed to get credit for their records. If you look at the label on a recent record, you will see a credit line for the record producer. You can reach him by addressing your letter to him in care of the record company. All his mail is forwarded to him. If you are writing to ask for permission to submit your songs, which is the proper thing to do, you will find in most cases that permission will be granted. Make certain that you bring or mail *both* your lead-sheets and demos. Go get 'em!

15

MEETING THE ENTERTAINERS

Now that I have tried to explain all the reasons for your seeing the A&R men at the various record companies, don't overlook the artists and the entertainers signed with *other* record labels. This is a *must!* They have the biggest voice in choosing the songs.

These entertainers are constantly on the move, so try to find out where and when they will be appearing in your vicinity. The entertainment sections of your local newspapers and the important trade magazines such as *Variety* list the nightclubs, theaters, concerts, colleges, universities, fairgrounds, and anywhere else an artist may be appearing.

Patronize these places and try to get to meet these artists personally. These entertainers will appreciate your showing up, because by paying your way in you will add to the crowds watching their performances. In this way you're contributing to their popularity and helping them, even though in actuality you are there to try to get them to help you.

Once you do get the opportunity to meet the artists don't force the issue. Remain courteous at all times. Even if they refuse your material, remain on friendly terms, thanking them cheerfully for their time, because you will be approaching them again. Perhaps in the near future your songs won't be refused. Always think of the future when you're dealing with anyone who can eventually help you by singing your song.

Here's a little tip on tact that helped me. It is wise to get copies of those songbooks mentioned earlier, or copies of the trade mags, or teen magazines that are always writing stores about the top, the popular, and the up-and-coming recording artists. Use the knowledge gleaned from these write-ups on those who will be appearing in your area. If you can get an insight into them before you set out to meet them, you will be able to approach the artists on a more knowledgeable and friendly basis.

If an entertainer was originally from your city, the "local" angle could be a good opener for your conversation and prove to be a valuable selling point. Better still, if you are a prolific writer and can write songs in many different styles, you should find out which songs were the artist's previous hits and study them carefully. If you are able to pattern your songs after those that brought the artist success, you can approach them by saying you have written a definite follow-up to their previous song hits. Your chances of their being interested in hearing your song are excellent.

Try to see as many of the recording artists as your time and money allows, leaving your songs with all of them for consideration and possible use. Not only will it improve your odds, but you may be fortunate enough to have more than one of them record your song.

On the other side of the coin, promising the artist an *exclusive* is a method I've used in selling a song successfully. This means telling the artist that you won't show the song to anyone else until a decision is reached on it. This is a persuasive inducement for the artist to accept your song, and it has led to many of my songs being recorded.

16

COLLABORATION

Now that I have told you about some of the most important contacts you will have to make to start selling your songs successfully, you are probably telling yourself that you will never be able to do that much running around and writing. Take another logical step towards furthering your career by letting other brains go to work with you. Whether it is with one person or a group, two (or more) heads are better than one, as the saying goes.

More than ninety percent of today's song hits, as well as the standards of yesteryear, were written by collaboration. The greatest standard of all time, "Stardust," was written by Hoagy Carmichael *and* Mitchell Parish. Some of the biggest musical shows of stage and screen were written by the prolific collaborating team of Rodgers and Hammerstein. *My Fair Lady* had the winning combination of Lerner and Loewe, Rodgers and Hart comprise just one more team on a list of successful collaborators whose names could fill the pages of this chapter. All were formed because each had something to contribute to make for a winning collaboration.

Many songwriters are not qualified to write both words and music professionally. Victor Herbert, who wrote some of our most beautiful and popular musical operettas, never wrote the words to any of them. His most memorable works were written in collaboration with one lyric writer or another.

A legend in collaboration is the team of Brian Holland, Lamont Dozier, and Eddie Holland. They maintain they were simply trying to keep up with their boss Berry Gordy Jr.'s seemingly insatiable appetite for hit songs when they worked as Motown Records' wonder team. They penned such smash hits as "Nowhere to Run," "Same Old Song," "Can't Help Myself," "Heatwave," "Quicksand," "Jimmy Mack," and hundreds of other titles. Their collaboration on hit songs for The Supremes alone was enough on which to base a successful songwriting team. The hits of the 60s are the standards of today—songs like "Where Did Our Love Go," "Stop In The Name Of Love," "Baby Love," and "You Keep Me Hanging On." According to Eddie Holland, their songwriting team worked because "you always had someone there to take over when your idea reached a dead end."

"Collaboration," said Lamont Dozier, "means just that. You have to enter a team with a democratic frame of mind."

They went on to explain that they were always competing with other songwriters. Berry Gordy jr.'s philosophy was that the best songs got recorded; he didn't care *who* wrote them. He was also writing songs for his firm and competing with them.

The Holland, Dozier and Holland collaboration team was inducted into the New York-based Songwriters' Hall Of Fame, and they were recipients of the national Academy Of Songwriters' second annual Lifetime Achievement Award.

Collaboration can give you the opportunity to concentrate on your main forte. It is an important link to your selling songs successfully. I myself am basically a lyric writer, although I can do both; and my song "Call Off The Wedding" was written in collaboration with Tom Glazer, who is a noted folksinger and children's storyteller. Another song, "Repeat After Me," was written with an important songwriter-music publisher, Fred Stryker. "Echo," which sold one quarter million records, was a collaboration by The Emotions, whose recording of it I produced.

Collaboration can bring unlimited possibilities, freeing you to work on and improve your key talent. If you are a lyricist, find a good melody-writer; and if you are stronger on writing melodies, try to find an equally strong lyricist. There must be a happy and perfect "wedding" between you and your partner to form a lasting team. The blend must be there if harmony is to prevail.

A top songwriter and C&W singer, Marty Stuart, said that although he enjoys the challenge of writing alone, he has also come to savor the relationships formed through cowriting. Marty Stuart stated: "There's a thing about taking an idea, a piece of paper, a pencil and a guitar and sitting down with someone. Once you've written a song with somebody, you've forged a friendship that will last an eternity!"

If at all possible, find a collaborator who lives near you. You might find one among the bands you hear at one of the affairs you attend. Or you could try the music studios or music schools in your area, since many of their students are definitely interested in songwriting and may also be looking for a collaborator. If you happen to live near recording studios, pay them a visit and check the bulletin boards. Perhaps a band member is also looking for a collaborator. If you connect with one, you won't have to look for a band to make your demos, saving a lot of expense.

Being nearby allows you to get together more frequently with your collaborator, making it easier to iron out the kinks in your song. Of course, don't let this general rule stop you from finding a collaborator elsewhere, if you can't find one nearby. Mail collaboration has often worked successfully for me; and you can do it with a simple, inexpensive tape recorder.

If your search for a collaborator takes you away from home, look through the classified ads of trade mags, local newspapers, song books, and writer's magazines under the listing for "Songwriters" or "Songwriter/Collaborator." If not successful here, *you* put an ad in any of these places under the same listings, asking for a sample of their work on a cassette. If you are a lyricist, send a sample of your lyrics to your respondents so they can put a melody to it, tape it on a cassette, and mail it back to you for consideration. You can reverse this procedure if you write the melodies only. A cassette recorder can be as important a tool for the songwriter as his pencil and paper.

An important note here is that there must be a working agreement between you and your collaborator. There should be a fifty-fifty share of royalties from the songs produced. This will also include sharing the costs on everything, including the lead-sheets, a good demonstration record, mailing costs, and all other costs agreed on mutually. Trust in each other's talents and *respect* for each other's ideas are essential for a successful collaboration. TIP: Focus on and build on human potentials—yours and others!

17

SONGWRITER'S CLUBS AND CUSTOM RECORDINGS

Knowledge, drive, and the ability to take criticism and be self-critical are some of the other things people can help you with. Many others trying to make it as songwriters have gotten together to form beneficial associations in which they discuss their trials and errors in the music field.

You should be able to find these associations known as *songwriter's clubs* in or near your community. These are the meeting places where you can usually find some neophytes who can help you practice some of the tricks, traits, and tact you have been reading about in these pages. These clubs are formed for the express purposes of bringing together the beginners, oft-tried, the near and successful talent for the exchange of ideas and suggestions to further their careers.

By all means, *join* one of these songwriter's clubs. Newspapers sometimes run ads from clubs seeking new members; and most of the monthly magazines catering to writers of poems, books, lyrics, and songs occasionally run such ads. Try to find and choose one that meets within travelling distance and charges dues within your means. You can also find the ones more to your liking and needs by sending for their literature and reading about their criteria and what they offer to their membership. Then, if at all possible, attend some of their meetings before choosing. When you do make your choice, choose the one that corresponds to your needs and seems to offer you the most help in reaching your goals.

Listen carefully to what each member has tried in the field. Adapt those tactics that brought success and put them to use for yourself. Don't be afraid to accept criticism. Learn to value others' opinions. No one is infallible. Others may uncover or discover errors in your work and working that you have overlooked. Follow advice if it is unanimous and sounds logical. It may be the difference between a near sale or selling your song successfully.

If there are no songwriter's clubs in your area that meet your needs, take it upon yourself to form one. You will find that there are many friends and neighbors with other friends and acquaintances who would be glad to join once you take the initiative. Many people have songs for sale. If you all band together towards a mutual furthering of your talents, you will succeed. Learn from others, work with others, and prosper!

Songwriter's clubs can lean you into an ideal situation for selling your songs via "group participation." If the publishers, artists, and record companies haven't as yet shown any interest in seeing your material, you must seek a way to promote your talents and make them sit up and take notice. Your song must be heard, and you only accomplish this with a recording. Nothing happens today unless a recording of your song is played and heard.

We recommend that a group of songwriters (members of your club) band together for a recording project which is too costly for one person to undertake. If shared by many, the expenses will be negligible and the gamble worthwhile. A commercial pressing of your songs on a record with your own label may run into several thousand dollars, with you supplying the artists, furnishing the recording studios, and producing enough copies of your finished recording for promotion.

To save you running around to look for the artists, musicians, and recording studios, and to get a complete pressing of your commercial records, you can turn to custom recording studios, which specialize in the growing business of making commercial recordings. A commercial recording means a polished master recording of your songs in a quality studio with the use of their professional vocalists and a band that is formed by four or more union musicians. A songwriter can get his songs recorded, mastered, processed, and pressed, all in one neat package that can save you thousands of dollars. You can find these studios in your classified telephone directory under "CUSTOM RECORDINGS."

A good way to decide on which studio will come up with the best work for you is to ask for a sample recording of their work. Specify the type and style recording you are particularly interested in. Enclose a dollar or two to cover their mailing costs, and remember to request the prices for their services. You want a good product to sell and you want it wrapped in the best packaging possible so that it will be presented in a professional manner. This is the growing, modern trend for today's songwriters.

Remember that you and your club will be absorbing the costs of all this by pooling your funds. The first songs for the recording session should be chosen in a fair manner. It is only natural for you to want your song chosen, but the recording company you have selected should make the choice, since they will pick impartially from the songs submitted, without knowing who wrote them. Also, since the names of their artists and band will be on the finished product, they will definitely look for the songs they feel could make it in today's market.

Don't feel badly if your song isn't one of the first chosen for the initial recording session. You should all agree beforehand that the pooled money will be used eventually to record at least one song from every member. Of course, you can accomplish this easily and economically by putting the songs into an album.

If your first recording session produces a record that sells well enough to absorb the cost, it can only benefit all the members and inspire you all to continue further. More importantly, the first recording can help you make valuable contacts for your next record session, making it easier for you to record your own song on your own or with a collaborator.

18

PROMOTION

Notice that two-thirds of *promotion* is *motion!*

A record has become the only way to really promote your talent. In today's modern approach to selling songs, the record is in the driver's seat. So the only logical way to start your song off by yourself is by promoting your record.

Music publishers are becoming the last people to see by songwriters because they also have to secure a recording of copyrighted sheet music if it is going to mean anything to them. They find themselves in your position, except you did what I spoke about in the preceding chapter—you had a recording made on your own. True, you paid for your custom recording, but you were wise enough to know that without a recording, your chances would be slim that anything would happen soon to your song.

With the record in your hand, you don't have to have an " in" or know anybody. Your record must do the talking for you, with your determined help in promoting it. Your efforts don't end with the recording of your song. You can't afford to sit back and wait for something to happen. You must make it happen. There are many steps you can take to do this, using your record as a "pivot" point.

The life of your song will depend on the strength of your record so make it the best possible advertisement for your song and the best publicity factor for your songwriting. Your record should be passed around to as many people in the trade as possible. You should also send copies to the trade magazines, with a nice letter about yourself asking them to review your record for commercialism. In this way you will be able to notify the trade that a new songwriter has appeared on the record scene. Those VIPs in the music trade always scour the record reviews, keeping their eyes open for new talent. This type of promotion pays off when a record company reads a highly favorable review and contacts you to "buy" your record. It means a promotion of your record, thereby assuring you some measure of success. Also, if the record company doesn't have a music publishing branch, another publisher will come after you for the publishing rights to your song and offer you an advance to sign with them.

Many songs have a long history of being passed up by the trade, only to become hits through the songwriter's sheer determination. This possibility alone should certainly make it worth the effort you put into your promotional activities.

Now let us move on to the most important way of promoting a record today. In the early 1900s, the music business was simple enough. Most songwriters who were selling songs successfully became what was known as "songpluggers." This meant that the songwriter went to all the theaters, cabarets, and various chain stores where music was being sold, and proceeded to sing his songs as best he could to the people gathered there. What he was doing was promoting his song and trying to create a demand for it.

In this ever-changing world, the name *song-plugger* has been replaced by a breed of supersalesman called promotion men. Their key markets have become the radio stations. *Nothing* happens to a record today without airplay; so one of the most important factors in the song market is radio promotion. The recording of your song must be exposed to gain any sort of recognition and a chance to become a hit. So you must become a "promotion man"; and just like him, you must know that the most important intermediary between your record and the music-buying public is the discjockey.

To reach these disc jockeys, you must try to cultivate a friendship with radio stations, or at least get them to know you. A good promotional start is to equip yourself with at least several hundred good-quality recordings of your song. Start by concentrating in your local area, making it your it "testing" site. Most records are tested in the smaller stations. Based on telephone response and sales at local record stores, these stations begin to establish which songs their audiences like. Once the smaller stations have put the new records through a "strainer," the larger stations begin to play the records. That way, the big stations are not gambling; they are playing a proven record. That record then becomes a smash hit because it is played on the major stations. The larger radio stations thus become responsible for and credited with selling million-plus records.

Radio stations are usually more receptive to local talent and are often willing to at least listen to your record and evaluate it for possible airplay. CAUTION: As you know from listening to your favorite radio stations, each features a certain type of music. So, if your record features a song arranged with a lot of "strings" and is what you would call a smooth, standard-type ballad, you should concentrate on those stations that feature "good-listening music." If your song has a raucous rock beat, you should go after your rock stations. If your song has the "contemporary," popular music sound of today, by all means concentrate on the stations that feature this type of music. If you classify your record as "country" or "folk," go after the country and western stations. In this way, you will eliminate immediate rejection, dejection, and embarrassment.

After you have thoroughly studied and finally chosen only those radio stations that cater to your type record, you should visit their record libraries and ask to meet the record librarians, music directors, or disc jockeys. When you do get to meet them, ask them politely to please help you get a start with your songwriting career by playing your record. Impress on them the "local talent" advantage. The "local-boy-makes-good" angle on selling yourself makes good publicity for the station and you. Let them know that you would be glad to cooperate in any way to promote their station as well, including an on-the-air interview to talk about your new record and your songwriting career to add live humaninterest to their program and please their listening audience.

The "local boy" angle worked with me when I started out to promote a new group I had recorded and whose songs I collaborated on. My record was turned down by ten major companies before I connected with a new, growing record company and a radio station that loved my "local-boy-makes-good" story. The group was the Emotions and the song "Echo" went on to hit #1 on their station and a quarter-million record sales in the New York area alone. The radio station was WMCA, which helped launch many new artists and songs. The disc jockeys there were appropriately named "The Good Guys," and among them were Harry Harrison, Dan Daniels, and Ed Bear, all of whom are now located at other top music stations in the New York area. So keep looking and plugging away, and you too will surely find YOUR "good guys."

Assuming that your humility and sincerity reach through to the disc jockeys and they finally consent to play your record at least once or twice for reaction, it is then up to you to follow through with a concerted effort of ftirther promotion. Convince your relatives and ftiends to get their postal cards, letters, and phone calls into the station, commenting on how much they like your song and want to hear it again.

TIP: You, too, should send in cards and letters, using different names and addresses and making your calls under assumed names and voices if at all possible. Although most radio stations know where most of the mail and calls are coming from, they will still be appreciative of the many people who, while willing to help you, are also tuning into their programs to listen for your song. That's how radio stations get high ratings, and high ratings are what makes radio stations large. A radio station with high ratings becomes an important part of the music business because they get advertisers who are willing to spend more money.

Often the disc jockeys and radio stations in your local area will pass on playing your record the first time around, but don't let it get you down. They will eventually have to play your record once you are able to promote your action successfully in another area and it works its way back home again.

Should any radio station ever tell you that it would not play your song unless it came from an "agency affiliate" you should file a complaint with the proper government organizations such as the Federal Communications Commission and the Federal Trade Commission, both located in Washington, DC. These agencies will see to it that you are treated fairly and not illegally by radio stations.

You should expand your record promotion to take in the stations within a one hundred to two hundred mile radius, especially if they are within reach of your radio receiver. In this way, you can tune in various stations to hear if they are giving your record any airplay. If your record is being played, your efforts are starting to pay off and all is not lost. Your promotional activities may also entitle you to some earnings in the form of *performance royalties* (see following chapter).

Let us assume that your first record attempt has received only a smattering of airplay and reaction; and except for some small performance royalties, if any, nothing of great importance has happened to your first effort to make the music trade beat a path to your door. You are now rightfully feeling let down, and your sagging spirits have made you run out of enthusiasm and hustle. *Stick to it.* You have gained valuable experience and learned some important lessons; and in the process of spending your time, effort, and money, you have finally projected yourself into the music business. Although you have now learned that it can be a bitter business fraught with disappointments, take heart in knowing that eventually it all will be sweetened with sales. REMEMBER: Whoever has never tasted what is bitter does not know what is sweet!

Think of your limited experience in promoting your record as a need for further experience. You will learn that promotion is a separate phase of this business and it requires the same effort and concentration that you give to your songwriting. In fact, there are people in the music business who devote themselves exclusively to promotion and are hired by record companies for that sole function. They reap huge dividends from this important selling function and rightfully so.

Although you may not have had any success to speak of as a promotion man, the knowledge and contacts you will have established from your efforts will come in handy when you finally do start clicking and the music trade gets to know that you are out there selling your songs. They will recall you from previous encounters, especially if you were wise enough to leave them with a good impression and good will. If your promotional efforts really struck home, you will be remembered and welcomed next time around, when they will be more than willing to help you continue on your way to selling songs successfully.

To illustrate to you that a good promotional effort can have a lasting effect on those you come in contact with, here's an anecdote I often tell. A woman shopper walks into a large supermarket and says to the manager, "I'm sorry I don't remember the brand right now—but I can hum a few bars of the commercial!"

19

PERFORMANCE ROYALTIES and CLEARANCE SOCIETIES

Through your promotion efforts, you may be lucky enough to receive airplay from the radio stations, entitling you to performance royalties. But many songwriters fortunate enough to have their songs released on commercial records that receive considerable airplay don't know about, or belong to, a *clearance society*. These songwriters are foolishly losing money that is due them.

If you're not familiar with this phase of the music business, you should know that money is earned for your songs principally through performance royalties—money paid to songwriters who are members of a performing rights society. These clearance societies give radio, TV, and all commercial places featuring music the right or clearance, for a *fee* to perform their members' songs without violating the songs' copyrights.

Under copyright law, an artist cannot perform or play somebody else's music for profit without first obtaining permission. When a song or a piece of music is used as part of a service provided by any business, payment for the use must go to those entitled to receive it.

ASCAP and BMI are the intermediaries or clearance societies in this transaction, acting as stewards for monies collected and paid!

Nightclubs, theaters, shows, radio and television, and all commercial places are using music for profit, so these outlets are required to pay for this use. ASCAP and BMI give them the necessary clearance and, in turn, collect the fees for their members. In essence, they act as your agents. All of these proceeds are then divided among the concerned songwriters who are affiliated with ASCAP or BMI. This performance money is the prime source from which any songwriter accrues his annuities. Most writers and publishers could not stay in business without them.

If you get good results and continue to produce more songs, you should have no difficulty being accepted for membership. Once you do become a a member, it is up to you to continue producing more songs and getting them performed at outlets licensed by ASCAP or BMI. By getting more and more performances on your songs, you will have a higher income and possibly a lifetime annuity.

When you start earning your way in your chosen performance rights society, you will be making money in one of the most important arenas of the music business. To help you choose the performing rights society that is best for you, here are the most important questions and answers regarding "What It Is," "Who It Is," and "How It Works."

Q. WHAT IS *ASCAP*?
A. ASCAP is the American Society of Composers, Authors and Publishers. It was founded in New York in 1914 and is the oldest performing rights licensing organization in the U.S. It is a membership organization which distributes to its members all income—after deducting operating costs. It's an organization of composers, lyricists, and music publishers. The word *Author* in the name stands for lyricists. It's the only U.S. performing rights organization owned and run by its writer and publisher members.

Q. WHY WAS *ASCAP* FOUNDED?
A. So that the creators of music would be paid for the public performances of their works, and users (licensee) could comply with the federal copyright law.

Q. HOW DOES AN *ASCAP* LICENSE WORK?
A. ASCAP licenses the non-exclusive right to perform publicly all copyrighted music works of members. ASCAP was created to establish a simple, practical, and economical licensing system. The ASCAP license gives the right to use any and all of the works of any and all of their members as often as the license holder wants. just as a copyright owner would find it impossibly difficult and expensive to locate and license every user, it would be just as difficult and costly for a bulk user to search out thousands of copyright owners across the country and negotiate separate licenses for each of the many works performed. Thus, ASCAP is an immensely useful organization for music creators and users. ASCAP licenses all kinds of music, and their members contribute to the whole spectrum of American music. They license the right of nondramatic performance in public of many copyrighted musical works of thousands of members under U.S. copyright

law. Under the law, public performances of copyrighted musical compositions without permission are unlawful unless exempted. ASCAP collects license fees from music users on behalf of the membership. Licensing non-dramatic performance rights in music is the only function.

Q. WHAT ELSE CAN MEMBERS EXPECT?

A. ASCAP protects their thousands of composers, lyricists, and publishers against unauthorized public performances by unlicensed users. They track performances of members' works through a sampling survey system designed and supervised by independent experts. ASCAP collects fees and distributes royalties for public performances in the U.S. and abroad. They further offer workshops, scholarships, and awards to encourage new writers and reward excellence. They make available literature on the Society and general aspects of the business. ASCAP works to protect the rights of music creators in the courts and in Congress against attacks on their copyrights.

Q. HOW DOES IT COLLECT FEES AND DISTRIBUTE ROYALTIES?

A. ASCAP's collection of license fees is divided into two operations: broadcast licensing and general licensing. The general licensing division collects fees from all licensees other than broadcasters. After ASCAP's operating costs are paid and amounts are set aside for foreign societies, half of the remainder goes to the writer members and the other half to the publisher member. Each group has its own distribution formula. The key factor in both royalty distribution systems is the number and kind of performances logged in ASCAP's survey. This is a scientifically designed survey of performances on AM and FM radio, local and network television, public broadcasting, cable TV, airlines, Muzak and similar background services, live performances in symphony and concert halls, colleges and universities, the Disney ice shows, and Ringling Brothers circuses. The survey and its operation are reviewed and evaluated regularly and the reports are sent to ASCAP's entire membership. Under this objective system for crediting members, all members are treated equally. There are no "special deals."

Q. HOW DO I *JOIN ASCAP?*
A. To become a writer member, you need either a commercially recorded musical composition, or a musical composition for which sheet music has been made available for sale in regular commercial outlets; or a musical composition performed in media licensed by ASCAP. To join, send proof of your eligibility (e.g., copy of a record or sheet music) along with a signed application for membership to the ASCAP Membership Department. Write them for the application. It does not cost anything to join. There is no initiation fee. Annual dues are only $10 for writers. New members are always welcomed.

Q. WHERE IS *ASCAP* LOCATED?
A. ASCAP headquarters are located:

In New York
ASCAP Building
I Lincoln Plaza
New York, NY 10023

In Los Angeles
ASCAP
7920 Sunset Blvd.
Los Angeles, CA 90046

In Nashville
ASCAP
2 Music Square West
Nashville, TN 37203

Q. WHAT IS *BMI*?
A. Broadcast Music Incorporated, more popularly known as BMI, is a music performing rights organization.

Q. WHAT IS A PERFORMING RIGHT?
A. It is the rizht zranted under the U.S. Copyright Act to owners of musical works to license these works to be publicly performed in places such as radio and TV stations and networks, cable TV and radio operations, nightclubs, hotels, discos, and other establishments that use music in an effort to make or enhance their profit.

Q. DOES *BMI* HANDLE ALL THESE RIGHTS?
A. No; BMI handles only performing rights.

Q. WHAT DOES *BMI DO*?
A. There are thousands of radio stations, TV stations, hotels, nightclubs, and other places in the U.S. which perform music publicly for profit. It would be virtually impossible for an individual to license these himself/herself. Therefore BMI acquires rights from authors, composers, and publishers and, in turn, grants licenses to use its entire repertory to users of music. BMI collects fees from each user of music it licenses. It is their objective to distribute to their writers and publishers all the money they collect, other than what is needed for operating expenses.

Q. HOW DOES *BMI* KEEP TRACK OF PERFORMANCES ON RADIO AND TELEVISION?

A. Because there are so many local radio broadcasting stations, it is impossible to keep track of everything each one of them plays every day of the year. Instead, a scientifically chosen representative cross section of stations is sampled each quarter. The stations being sampled supply BMI with complete information as to all music performed. These lists, known in the industry as logs, are put through an elaborate computer system which multiplies each performance listed by a factor which reflects the ratio of the number of stations logged to the number licensed. BMI logs approximately 500,000 hours of commercial radio programming annually.

Non-commercial college radio is logged using the same methodology, with the more-than-50,000 hours of programming tracked resulting in separate payments for these performances.

Television feature, theme and cue music is logged with the aid of cue sheets, which list all music performed in the program. TV networks provide BMI with cue sheets for all network programming. All syndicated programs and motion pictures shown on local television are logged through information obtained through cue sheets and computerized data. Cable television is logged in a similar fashion.

Through cue sheets and computerized data BMI pays for all performances on network, syndicated, and cable television on a true census basis, keeping track of over 6,000,000 hours of programming annually.

Q. HOW ARE MY ROYALTIES COMPUTED?
A. BMI uses a system similar to that of other performing rights organizations throughout the world and considers payments to writers and publishers as a single unit equal to 200%. Where there is the usual division of performance royalties between writer(s) and publish-

ers, the total writer(s)' share will be 100%, (1/2 of the available 200%) and the total publishers' share will be the remaining 100%. The rates described are base rates and constitute a 200% share. Because BMI operates on a nonprofit basis, they may distribute all available income, and may, from time to time, voluntarily pay increased royalties to their writers and publishers BMI publishes a payment schedule of performing rights royalties. A copy of this schedule is given to you when you affiliate with BMI. If BMI should change its payment structure, a revised schedule will be sent to you.

Q. HOW OFTEN DO I GET PAID?
A. Statements for broadcast performances in the U.S. and Canada are rendered to their affiliates four times each year. Statements reflecting foreign royalties are rendered semi-annually. Statements relating to live concert performances are rendered once a year.

Q. HOW DOES *BMI* KNOW WHAT WORKS SHOULD BE PAID FOR?
A. BMI supplies you with "clearance forms" on which you give them all relevant information with respect to each song you write, such as the name of the co-writer(s), the publisher, etc. This information enables BMI to identify the works for which you are entitled to payment.

Q. WHO IS ELIGIBLE TO AFFILIATE WITH *BMI* AS A WRITER?
A. If you have written a musical composition, alone or in collaboration with other writers, and the work is either commercially published, recorded, or otherwise likely to be performed, you are eligible to apply for affiliation with BMI.

Q. WHY SHOULD ONE AFFILIATE?
A. Because if your works are being performed and you do not affiliate, BMI will be unable to pay you the performance royalties your song would earn.

Q. DOES *BMI* TAKE CARE OF PERFORMANCES OUTSIDE THE U.S. AND CANADA?
A. Yes. BMI has agreements with all important performing rights societies in foreign countries. If a work of yours is played, for example, in England, the British performing rights society will collect there and transmit the money to BMI for your account.

Q. MAY I COLLABORATE WITH A WRITER WHO IS NOT AFFILIATED?
A. Yes. However, your collaborator will have no way to collect performance royalties of your jointly written work unless he affiliates with BMI.

Q. MAY I COLLABORATE WITH AN *ASCAP* WRITER?
A. Yes!

Q. CAN I *JOIN ASCAP* WHILE AFFILIATED WITH *BMI*?
A. No. A writer may not affiliate with more than one licensing organization, foreign or domestic, at the same time.

Q. WHAT IS THE DURATION OF A USUAL *BMI* CONTRACT?
A. Two years. At the end of the term, the contract is automatically renewed unless either you or BMI gives notice 60 days before the termination of the contract.

Q. MAY I WRITE UNDER A PSEUDONYM?
A. Yes. If yours is a very common name such as John

Smith, or Jones, or if you have a name hard to pronounce, it is often better to use a pseudonym as a means of surer identification. Be certain to list all your pseudonyms on your application. List your proper address as well. If you move, send in your new address immediately. This will ensure you will receive royalty statements and checks promptly.

Q. IF MY NAME IS LISTED INCORRECTLY OR LEFT OUT, WILL I LOSE PERFORMANCE ROYALTIES?

A. NO! If an error has been made on a record label or in a trade paper, you should promptly notify both BMI and the record company or trade paper involved. If you do this, and if you have properly submitted the clearance forms previously described, no error in record label copy or trade paper listing can affect your royalty payments. It is the information given to BMI on the clearance forms submitted by both you and your publisher that enables BMI to identify your works and pay for performances.

Q. DOES *BMI* PROVIDE OTHER SERVICES FOR WRITERS?

A. (1) BMI maintains the BMI-Lehman Engel Musical Theatre Workshop. Workshops are held in New York City. Admission to the sessions is determined by audition and the judgment of a board of workshop directors. There is no cost to the writer.

(2) For those interested in film and television music, BMI conducts the Earl Hagen Workshop. Further information can be obtained from the Film and Television Department in BMI's Los Angeles office.

(3) The BMI jazz Composers Workshop is available to those interested in that area of music. For further information, contact BMI's New York office.

(4) BMI publishes a magazine, BMI *Music World,* which illustrates the organization's multiple interests and achievements, offering insightful profiles of both established and up-and-coming composers.

(5) BMI Awards to Student Composers Competition. To encourage and aid young composers of concert music, BMI annually holds this competition and presents cash awards to the winners.

(6) BMI is actively engaged in working for improved copyright laws and similar matters of importance to creators and publishers of music.

(7) BMI also organizes and sponsors workshops and seminars, and actively participates in music events throughout the country. Contact the Writer/Publisher Relations Department for BMI-sponsored events in your area.

Q. WHAT DOES IT COST TO JOIN?
A. Nothing! BMI charges no fees or dues whatsoever to writers. You may write to BMI for application forms. New members are welcomed.

Q. WHERE IS *BMI* LOCATED
A. BMI headquarters are located:

In New York
BMI
320 West 57th Street
New York, NY 10019

In Los Angeles
BMI
8730 Sunset Blvd. (3rd floor)
Los Angeles, CA 90069

In Nashville
BMI
10 Music Square East
Nashville, TN 37203

20

THAR'S GOLD IN THEM THAR HILLS

Before we head for Broadway and the musical stage show scene, let's jump onto our horses and gallop off to the "hill" country in our search for the gold! The "hill" country, otherwise known as country and western territory, offers the new songwriters the easiest "break-in" market in terms of receptiveness and kindness towards new songs!

Perhaps the reason for this lies in the fact that so many of the country and western music publishers were, and still are, active songwriters; they are appreciative and can relate to the struggles and needs of the newer writers, and they openly solicit them.

But remember that today's country music is *not* the old country music. On today's recordings, the chord progressions are fuller and more "pop" in flavor. In a general musical sense, the country field has progressed considerably. As country music continues spreading, it increasingly influences the mainstream of "Pop" and other musical strains. This has resulted in a more sophisticated rhythm to the point where country music can now be called "modern" country and western.

The subject matter of today's country song hits is honest, earthy, and sincere. Country songwriters, in order to capture and hold the folk flavor, have to write about things they have felt or experienced. In that way, their songs are steeped with authentic emotion. Unfortunately, there are a limited number of emotions from which you can draw.

Remembering these qualities will help songwriters retain the nature and flavor of country material. You have to find different ways of saying "girl jilts boy," or "boy jilts girl," or "now I'm crying my eyes out for you." More than sixty percent of country and western songs are about love or broken love affairs; therefore, it stands to reason that if you were to base your songs on this subject, you will be at least sixty percent on your way in this C&W field toward *selling your songs successfully.*

Following the above criteria for writing C&W songs, I myself wrote a song titled "Call Off The Wedding" many years ago, which was recorded by a top C&W artist called "Goldie Hill, and covered in the 'pop' field by Sunny Gale. The lyrics said, "He promised to wed me, but then he mislead me. I am his true love, so call off the wedding." Of course, today I would say it differently, but it would still fit into the groove of country music's fondness for broken love affair songs.

Don Von Tress is a perfect example of an aspiring songwriter who knew how to tell, in a different and novel way, about how easy breaking up would be if your heart wasn't involved—and it helped him walk away with BMI's "Country Song Of The Year" award!

Don started writing the song at his sister's house for fun. It was a humorous look at life and Don said, "The lines just kept coming and if nothing else happened with the song, I certainly got a good laugh when I was writing it!"

The song was first recorded by the Marcy Brothers and it was originally titled "Don't Tell My Heart." To make the song more in keeping with the song-market, they changed the 'hook', a term for an oft-repeated 'catchy refrain', to "MY ACHY BREAKY HEART!"

When the song didn't go anywhere, two producers were approached by one of Don's 'contacts' to record this song with an unknown singer from Flatwoods, Kentucky. The singer was Billy Ray Cyrus and "Achy Breaky Heart", written by a former wallpaperer, went on to sell over NINE MILLION recordings, launched the sale of over SEVEN MILLION albums and hit number one on charts all over the world!

Country music fans are more selective and demanding now, so the songwriter can't write, "The sky is blue, I sure love you," anymore. Country music has been elevated in recent years by eliminating the word *hillbilly*. Many felt this word had a bad connotation, that it referred to all country music fans as country "bumpkins." C&W listeners today are better educated. Among the people who like country music now are bank presidents, college professors, doctors, lawyers, and computer programmers. To impress these intelligent listeners, you will have to write intelligent lyrics.

Amazingly, most C&W songwriters compose their hits within twenty minutes to one hour. These writers state that they write fast in order to retain the simplicity and feel of the song once they get the idea. But it is the idea that may take them days or weeks to come up with.

Many top songwriters get their ideas from all sorts of places, including the signs and billboards that line the highways. If a saying or a phrase strikes them, they quickly appropriate it for a song. In fact, Roger Miller, who wrote and won awards for his big hit song "King Of The Road," has said that the idea for the song came from a sign on a barn he spotted as he was riding by. The sign read, "Trailers for rent or sale." The opening lyrics of his hit song start with similar words.

A top C&W songwriter named Kostas Lazarides, known as Kostas in the music field, has stated: "You don't have to live in Nashville. You can write songs in a jail cell—you can write songs in a hospital bed."

When asked about the sources of his songs, Kostas replied: "It's everything from the political arena to the Vietnam War to male-female relationships, to between-male friendships, to dogs, trucks, trains and flying saucers, pine trees, elk, rivers, mountains, blue skies and stars, angels and devils! "

He then added: "All those things and every breath you take, every heartbeat, all those things!"

Other songwriters state that they get their ideas from listening to radio or television. Sometimes they find them by reading newspapers and magazines. At other times they sit around and tickle the keys of their piano, or strum on the guitar, hoping to hit upon an idea.

One songwriter said: "I get a lot of ideas for song titles while driving, so I keep a cassette near me in the car. I make a list of these titles, and I must have literally *thousands* of them. Whenever I sit down to write a song, I take out this list, look to see which title hits me good that day, and I work my song around it. I'm also always listening to what people say. I get a lot of ideas out of things people say in conversations."

As in the 'pop' field, many of the C&W songwriters can't read or write music, so they sing or play their songs into a tape recorder or cassette. They then proceed to play the song back to a music publisher. If the publisher likes what he hears, he has one of his staff arrangers make a lead-sheet copy of the song from the tape. Most C&W hits are written in this manner.

An abundance of recording talent available in this market makes an A&R man's job a difficult one. They now have so many artists for which they must find recording material that although they continue doing an excellent job, they cannot do justice in each individual case. This allows the artist freer play in his choice of recording material. Since the type, style, and feel of the song is most important to any artist, it stands to reason that nine out of ten times, the song chosen for the recording will be the one written by the artist—or at least one that they personally chose from another songwriter. So you can readily see why these C&W music publishers are worth going after. Since they are also artists in many cases, if they do accept your songs, you will almost be assured of a recording. If they encounter any difficulties in finding another artist to record your song, then in all probability, they will record it themselves.

With all these new influences affecting the country field, modern country now allows more songwriters to break in, where previously the field was restricted to the songwriters in Nashville, which is generally recognized as being the heart of country music. Now the arteries that lead to this heart, reach out from all over the country, pumping in new blood every day. To give you a chance to reach these most receptive C&W music publishers, I have listed some of them in the marketplaces section at the end of this book. As always, it is wise to write them first for permission to submit your material, enclosing return postage for their reply.

Thar's gold in them thar hills—*record* gold. And any aggressive, hustling songwriter can stake his claim in the C&W market.

21

THE MUSICAL STAGE SHOW

Now let us explore a very difficult market which is, nevertheless, worth going after because the performance royalties garnered in this field can reach astronomical proportions and lifetime annuities. For those of you fortunate enough to be gifted with the advance talent for writing plays or musical scores, there is a highly specialized and highly rewarding field awaiting you: THE MUSICAL STAGE SHOW.

The musical stage show can provide the songwriter with a weekly income of several thousand dollars while the show is being performed on Broadway or while it is touring the country. If the show is a hit with a running span of a year or more, the lucky, hard-working songwriter is almost guaranteed a lifetime annuity. And just think of the added riches if filming rights are bought by a movie company or if a recording company produces and releases an original-cast album.

Original-cast album recordings make an exceptional impact on sales because people are able to hear the songs exactly the way they are performed on stage. If they missed the show, they may buy the album as a substitute and then perhaps be further compelled to see the show, adding further to the songwriter's profits.

The musical score from *Oklahoma!* was the first original cast album to be successfully recorded by Decca Records in 1943. Since then, there has been competitive bidding for these original-cast album recording rights, with Columbia Records hitting the jackpot with *My Fair Lady*. To date, this is still one of the highest selling LPs of all time, along with *The Sound Of Music*. Both still continue to earn astronomical royalties for the writers.

Tune in your radio to any "good music" station and you will hear the airwaves filled with music from the various stage shows. In fact, some rock 'n' roll and contemporary stations are playing the single record releases of some of the tunes from the musical shows, interpreted in an upbeat manner by popular artists. The coverage is unlimited. The royalties involved make selling your songs to this market a worthwhile project for the truly ambitious songwriter.

Breaking into this expanding but difficult market offers a challenge that has been met by other talented and enterprising songwriters. Why not *you*? The best method is to get involved with a playwright who concentrates on musicals or whose plays can be worked into musicals. In this way, you can offer your services in writing either lyrics or music, or both, if he isn't interested in that end of the writing field. Or perhaps you will be fortunate enough to connect with a collaborator who is already at work on the score of a play in which he is doing the music and is seeking a lyricist, or vice versa. Still better, perhaps you are one of the really prolific songwriters who can do it all but has hesitated to do so before. Don't put it off. The dividends make it worthwhile.

Perhaps the plot has you baffled? The plots of most musical shows are only variations of well-tested formulas. In fact, two of the most successful stage shows, which won many musical awards when they were made into successful motion pictures, fit this category. *West Side Story* was based on Shakespeare's sad tale of *Romeo and Juliet*. It was altered for the current generation by adding teenage gang wars and bigotry. *My Fair Lady* was basically Pygmalion, which in turn was borrowed from the *Cinderella* fairy tale, in which a drab young girl is miraculously transformed into a radiant beauty. People love shows they are familiar with and can also identify with, and they will pay good money to see them.

One hit musical was successfully adapted from Mark Twain's books about life on the Mississippi River, featuring Tom Sawyer and Huckleberry Finn. It was called, appropriately enough, *Big River* by its writer Roger Miller, who also wrote the hit "King Of The Road." *Big River* was Miller's first attempt at a musical show and it won many awards. Once you have written your play or you have completed collaborating on one, you are probably anxious to be off and running to Broadway with it. But wait a while and think it over. How do you know if your show is ready for the market? When writing songs for the theater, both composer and lyricist must concentrate on being twice as visual as in any other medium. Every song has to move the plot along, reveal some hidden emotion, and remain faithful to the show's overall theme.

Will anyone go off humming or whistling your tunes? Do your lyrics weave in and out with the story to become an integral part of the plot? Is there one song too many or is there a gap that can be filled nicely with another song? Your lyrics must be crystal clear or they will impede your story line.

TIP: You have to feel out the prospects and get an audience reaction to your show. Always leave them wanting more and strive to understand what didn't work and why. *The next time you'll know better!*

You will find the answers to many of your unanswered questions in "tryouts." You should seek a tryout in the many places that are available to the new, unknown writer. Church functions sometimes offer this opportunity, if you can interest the entertainment committee in putting on your show for one of their fund-raising drives. Another showcase available to you is the amateur college acting groups, who aspire to reach Broadway or the movie screen. Convince them that your show has merits that can possibly help launch all their careers, and they will certainly consider doing it. The logical place for your tryout, if you can manage to get one, is an off-Broadway theater.

Big River had its tryout originally as a West Coast production before it made a successful move to Broadway. The tryout procedure has done a lot to encourage many young playwrights outside the New York area and has put the musical theater within the reach of many songwriters.

Many shows were seen off-Broadway by VIPs who then brought them to Broadway and further success. An example of an off-Broadway show going on to tremendous success was a little musical called *Hair!* This was a tribal, rock-love musical based on the "hippie manifesto." Although it became famous for its precedent-setting exposure of the human anatomy, its tunes culled *millions*. The show's most successful tune was a song called "Aquarius—Let The Sunshine In," a medley recorded by the Fifth Dimension which sold over three million records. Another million-seller from the show was "Good Morning Sunshine," by a new, unknown singer who went under the name Oliver. And still another million-seller was the title tune "Hair," recorded by the Cowsills. Many other artists also made it big by recording the songs from this musical stage show. The score from *Hair*, recorded by the original cast for RCA, also surpassed the million-seller mark and is still selling today. *Hair* has been called one of the most successful off-Broadway shows ever. It introduced three unknown songwriters who are no longer unknown, thanks to the musical theater and their learning how to sell their songs successfully in this field.

So you too should try to get your musical produced anywhere you can. Once you get someone to produce it, you will be able to learn more about the strengths and weaknesses of your writing and composing than you can learn anywhere else. Stay involved in the rehearsal process and try to get everyone involved as excited about doing your musical as you were about writing it.

Even when shows have been closed down, the songs from them have often gained recognition, having brought the songwriters to the attention of the music publishers and record companies. Yes, these same music publishers who ignored the songwriters' standard, popular, rock or C&W songs now attune themselves to the lucrative musical stage show field; and they have gone as far as the recording companies in now encouraging, cultivating, and financing many of the songwriters involved in the preparation of such shows.

The music publishers are now constantly on the prowl to sign writers, both established and *new*, m the hopes of cashing m on some of this musical stage show gravy. The record royalties and performance fees to be earned continue to be the big drawing attraction for the music publishers.

Much of the credit for opening the stage doors of Broadway belonged to an enthusiastic music publisher who broke out of the confines of Tin Pan Alley and took over Shubert Alley. This publisher, Tommy Valando, made it easier for the talented songwriter to break into a previously considered tough field to penetrate. Several songwriters he had faith in and continued to encourage and nurture through very trying periods finally paid him off in big dividends when they broke through with hits, including the very successful *Cabaret* and *Fiddler On The Roof*.

If this is your market for selling songs successfully, you should *study* the musical albums of the various stage shows and *pattern* your writings after them. Or if you are one of the really prolific and creative talents who writes both book and music, I suggest you *run* with your manuscript and demo in hand to any and all of the listed music publishers on your musical stage show albums. These publishers will definitely prove to be the most active and receptive and will help you find the backers and even invest themselves if they like what you have. Perhaps in the very near future, we will be seeing *your* show on Broadway and be listening to your songs on original-cast albums!

22

HOW TO SAVE MONEY COPYRIGHTING YOUR SONGS

There are always unscrupulous people in the music business who, after hearing your song, will try to alter or revise it slightly, borrow or appropriate a large part of it, or steal your entire song and then put their name to it. There is also the possibility that an honest person in the music business may steal your song unintentionally. Someone may read or hear your song, reject it, and inform you of the fact. Then, maybe days or weeks later, that person may find himself humming or singing your song. Thinking that the tune just popped into his head, he may work it up as his own. Normally, anyone who makes use of your song without your permission is liable under our laws to an injunction to restrain the infringement of the copyright and to a suit for damages.

What, then, does registration of your copyright do for you? It allows you to institute a lawsuit against anyone who infringes on your copyright, since you couldn't normally go into court without a registration certificate. It further serves to put record companies on notice as to who the copyright owner is for the purpose of obtaining statutory royalties for recording your song.

A copyright is a certification from the Copyright Office in the Library of Congress that you are the acknowledged writer of an original musical composition on a certain date. This is the lawful way to protect your songs. A copy of your song is filed as verification with the Copyright Office. You may apply, without charge, for these copyright forms by writing to and asking for application forms PA from:

REGISTER OF COPYRIGHTS
COPYRIGHT OFFICE
LIBRARY OF CONGRESS
WASHINGTON, DC 20559

These forms will come to you in duplicate, and you must fill them out as directed, providing all the information required. You must then attach a copy of your song (lead-sheet or piano copy) to your application; and with a check or money order for twenty dollars, mail it all back to the Copyright Office. Allow ten to sixteen weeks for the return of one of your copies as your official copyright.

A copyright registration is effective on the date all the required elements (application form, fee, and songs) in acceptable form are received in the Copyright Office, regardless of the length of time it takes the Copyright Office to process the application and mail the certificate of registration. You do not have to receive your certificate before you publish or produce your work, and you don't need permission from the Copyright Office to place a notice of copyright on your material.

This copyright gives you the right to control your song. No one can use any part of it without your permission. You can assign it to a music publisher if you wish or you can permit it to be used by anyone. This is what is meant by the "exclusive right" inherent in our copyright law.

If you intend putting out a commercial record on your own, you should also request and fill out the form on "sound recordings." Your application forms will tell you in detail what forms you must complete to protect yourself further under the copyright laws.

The year of copyright and the name of the copyright owner must appear on the song as proof of its ownership, or the song can be stolen from you. It should appear on the first page of your music, preferably at the bottom. If you look at the sample lead-sheet at the close of the chapter "Preparing Your Song," you will see where and how to enter the copyright data.

Perhaps the one thing about registration that upsets most writers today is the cost of $20 per song. But there is a way—a relatively inexpensive way—to protect a large number of songs. The Copyright Office will accept registration of an unpublished *collection of works* for a single $20 fee if all of the following requirements are met:

1. You put all the works together in an orderly manner with a single title. You can use any title describing the collection. For instance: "The songs of (your name)," or "Songs I have written," or any similar generality. If you send lead-sheets, you should fasten them together or put

them in a folder. However, you may send a recording or tape containing all your songs, instead.

2. The copyright claimant for every selection and the entire collection must be the same. This means you are claiming to be the copyright owner of each and every song.

3. All the selections in the collection must be by the same author, or if they are by more than one author, the author claiming copyright must have contributed copyrighted material to each selection.

Keep in mind that the Copyright Office will only register the title of your collection, not the individual titles of your songs. But there is still another way, for just another $20 payment, to get *each* song title registered. Once you receive the copyright registration certificate back for the collection, file FORM CA (Correction/Amplification), listing the individual titles in the collection, and the Copyright Office will then cross-reference the collection with the title of *every* song on it. In this way you can register ten, fifty, one hundred songs, for a total of only $40.

23

AVOIDING THE SONGSHARKS

Just as your song titles act as headlines to attract your audience, other kinds of headlines can be deceptive lures designed to pick your pockets. Headlines on advertisements devised to attract new songwriters may read something like these: "DO YOU WRITE SONGS? LET US RECORD AND PUBLISH THEM FOR YOU," or "SONGWRITERS EARN THOUSANDS WITH OUR HELP," or "LET US WRITE A HIT MELODY FOR YOUR POEMS OR LYRICS," and so forth and so on. I am certain you may have seen these ads in your search for help in your start of songwriting. They are devised by people who make offers they will seldom, if ever, be able to fulfill.

Stay away from these eye-catching ads and you will be avoiding the *songsharks*. You may be searching for an easy way to break into the music business, and you may be tempted by the attraction of a songshark's offer, and turn to him for help. But remember that these "operators" work on the theory that many new songwriters will pay considerable chunks of their hard-earned money just to see their name on a fancy sheet of music or a contract. These "operators" prey on writers who know little or nothing about the music business. *Avoid them!*

Never pay to have your songs "published." If you are looking for your name in print, the songsharks will certainly give you this—*and nothing more.* They will make *no* effort to "plug" or promote your song. The songshark knows that the material he has helped you write for a fee is of poor commercial quality. There are *no* royalties to be gained from this approach, and you are surely being taken.

Another thriving songshark scheme to separate the beginning songwriters from their money is the "melody-for-a-fee" plan. The songshark offers to write a melody for your poem or lyrics for a "small" amount, ranging anywhere from $25 to $100 to as much as $1,000 and more, depending on whether it includes a demo recording. Most of these hit-and-run operators turn these tunes out with no feeling or enthusiasm at all. In fact, they use basically the *same* melody over and over again, with the tune altered slightly each time to fit the pattern of the words submitted. These fly-by-nighters know their tunes are trite and worthless. After all, putting yourself in their shoes, would you sell a good melody for $25 or even $1,000 if you stood to make a hundred times that by using the tune yourself?

None of these songsharks ever sold a song they collaborated on, and they probably never will. They are known to everyone in the music business, so when a song comes in bearing their names or one of their many aliases, they are immediately and automatically rejected. They thrive on the uneducated and gullible songwriter who can be easily trapped and snared by their false promises or exaggerated claims. You must learn to spend your money wisely and where it will do the most practical good. If you *don't* waste your time and money on songsharks, you will never waste your songs.

In order to sell your songs successfully, you must not only know what you *should* do, but also what you *shouldn't* do. So remember this important rule for survival in the song-selling waters—stay *away from the songsharks!*

24

"ANGLES" AND MAKING DEALS

Hopefully, by now you have absorbed all of the practical information given to you to help sell your songs successfully. I must admit there have always been, and probably always will be, amateur songwriters making it, although they have gone contrary to the accepted practices outlined here. But there are also plenty of others who have made it even tougher for other songwriters to find an outlet for their songs, because of their continuous abuses of the accepted practices in this business.

You may pick up a paper one day and read about a new songwriter whose first effort was a hit overnight, and you may say to yourself, "If he can do it, why can't I?"

Remember one thing: A story such as this is meant to attract attention and interest. This "overnight" hit songwriter may in actuality have spent years trying to make it. He may have been wise enough to build up his contacts and then be able to turn to them years later. Or perhaps a relative was instrumental in getting him in to see the proper people. Or more likely, it was the classic case of being in the right place at the right time with the right song.

Also, one of the most overlooked phases of song-selling is the "wheeling and dealing" that goes on in this field. The music business has its "angles" too, just like any other business. You must learn how to "rock and roll" with the punches and accept it as part of the selling game. There are "deals" to be made, "cut-ins" to be offered; and fortunately or unfortunately, depending on how you look at it, these are *important* factors in selling songs successfully. As it was put to me by a top music publisher when I started out in the music business and he wanted to put one of his staff writers on my song: "Do you want 50 percent of *something* or 100 percent of *nothing?*"

I readily accepted the *fifty percent of something!* It helped open doors that were previously closed to me because I then had a major recording out by a major music publisher.

This also holds true today. Would you be willing to offer an important recording artist *half* of the royalties on your song? Would you be willing to have a music publisher's staff writer put his name on your song, even if his contribution to it was to add a few words that helped polish it? If your answer to these questions are "Yes," you won't be disappointed in the music business, and your outlook on life itself will be greatly improved.

Think of it this way: You'll be making an initial investment that can eventually gain you *bigger* dividends. Once you've gotten your foot in the door and the music trade gets to know you, *you* will be in a position to choose your "deals" and swing *your* "angles."

25

IMPORTANT DO's AND DONT's FOR SELLING SONGS SUCCESSFULLY

If you still feel that all you need do is write your song to have your hit, you are in for a disillusionment. Such cases are rare. That's why I wrote this book about *selling* songs rather than about writing them. If you are willing to follow what this book can teach you, you can only profit from it eventually.

New and unknown songwriters have always had difficulty getting their songs recorded. The main reason is that many songwriters don't bother to learn all they can about the trade and therefore handle themselves like amateurs. This in turn has made it almost impossible for the deserving and talented songwriters to break through.

If you are convinced you really have come up with a good song and have learned not to give up—learned to overlook rejection—then somewhere along the hard road ahead you are bound to run into someone who will see your possibilities. Talent and learning will always win out in the end.

If you really want to be a professional songwriter, you must always be on the lookout for ways to improve by reviewing what you have learned in the pages of this book and through other techniques. I have prepared an important list of DO's and DON'Ts that is certain to add a few new and inspiring thoughts for you. It can also serve as a reminder of successful selling strategies. If you refer to this list periodically, you will soon find yourself on the right path to profitable songwriting!

DO take the most important first step in selling songs—BEGIN! This field is wide open to those with talent, patience, fortitude, and the ability to learn.

DON'T start until you have first read and absorbed all the tricks, tact, and traits mentioned in this book.

DO put your best foot and efforts forward. If you are willing to put in the time, effort, and energy involved, you can expect to reach what you are striving for, especially if you expand on your talent.

DON'T just put any of your songs out to market simply because you wrote it. Unless you are truly satisfied that it is your very best effort, and unless you feel it is of professional quality, don't show it around. It will mark you as a beginner.

DO be enthusiastic about your song. Show others that you believe your song can become a hit, and convince them that you aren't wasting their valuable time in considering your effort.

DON'T be afraid to ask for opinions and advice. A person who has arrived in the music industry can teach you a great deal. If you can get the VIP talking, he may give you some worthy advice that can help you sell your next contact. Further, by your asking, you will be giving him a feeling of importance and self-worth, which will endear you to him and make for a valuable future contact.

DO get to know as many of your contacts' office staff as possible when calling in person. Be friendly. His assistant, secretary, office boy, and anyone in his organization can open doors for you and put in a good word for your songs.

DON'T barge in on any contact. Always call or write for an appointment. If you drop in unexpectedly, he is not likely to be in a receptive mood.

DO be prepared when calling on your contact. Is your appearance neat? Do you have a lead-sheet and demonstration record with you? Do you know why your song is worthy of a recording and why your contact should choose it over others he has listened to and liked?

DON'T be too insistent but be persistent. A well thought-out presentation can make a contact take notice and give your song the attention it deserves.

DO be concise. VIPs in the music business have limited time so their time is valuable. Make the most of the time they give you and you will make a friend.

DON'T argue with any of his decisions. Winning an argument but losing the VIP's respect doesn't produce a song sale and a valuable future contact.

DO be sincere. A genuine interest in the VIP and his company's success will be greatly appreciated. There is no stronger building block in a relationship than sincerity.

DON'T knock any one else's song, especially ones that your contact and the music industry have accepted and that your contact has had a hand in either recording or publishing them. It is far better to point out the good points in *your* song rather than run down the competitor's!

DO give yourself an edge over your competitors by searching for new faces and places to sell your song. Consider the artists' managers and booking agencies as a means of getting to them.

DON'T try to reach all of the various markets with many different types of songs. Find out what you are best at writing, whether it be contemporary songs, popular ballads, country and western, musicals, whatever, and concentrate on the markets in that particular field.

DO read this book again and again and do read these important DO's and DON'Ts for a better VIP relationship and to increase your odds for selling songs successfully.

DON'T make your job more difficult than it already is. Remember that the average person remembers 10% of what he hears, 30% of what he sees—but 50% of what he sees and hears simultaneously. So DON'T forget your lead-sheet with lyrics and your demonstration record for your presentation.

26

THE BASIC ABC's FOR SELLING SONGS SUCCESSFULLY

In elementary school, we were taught that the basis for learning to read and write was the alphabet. In song selling school, here are my basic ABCs for selling songs successfully:

A. **Aggressiveness** and hustle are the songwriter's greatest assets
B. **Beginners** should not submit their first efforts
C. **Collaboration** doubles your chances for success
D. **Demos** are a must for selling your songs
E. **Enthusiasm** is your springboard to success
F. **Follow-up** every possible lead if you want to get anywhere
G. **Getting** someone interested in your song requires skill and ingenuity
H. **Handle** yourself as a pro and you soon will become one

I. **Indie** record producers are always looking for new songs
J. **Jot** down ideas as they come to you; carry pad and pencil at all times
K. **Keep** your address list of artists and record companies up to date and handy for reference
L. **Lead-sheets** with your demos is the professional way for submitting your songs
M. **Master** recordings find ready listening at all record companies
N. **Note** your local talent because they can help you promote your songs
O. **Obey** the most important rule of always enclosing return postage with your mailings
P. **Persistence** pays off for the songwriters who just won't quit
Q. **Quack** songsharks doom your song efforts and get you an immediate rejection
R. **Records** are the prime requisite for making money on your songs
S. **Specialization** is a tactic that pays off for the clever and talented songwriter
T. **Titles** are the headlines of your song and the first contact for anyone
U. **Use** every trick, trait, and tact you have absorbed from reading this book
V. **Valuable** contacts can help you later on when you need them
W. **Write** letters first requesting permission to submit your songs
X. **Xtra** dividends for the songwriter who is also a performer
Y. **Youth** is still the main record market so write your songs for them
Z. **Zero** in on these basic ABCs for selling songs successfully

27

MARKETPLACES

The following pages contain my lists of many important marketplaces for you to visit or write. First on the list are the record companies and record producers, since without a recording of your song, there can be no song in today's market.

Although these lists have been researched, between the time of publication and you contact those listed, some may or may not still be active. That is why I always stress, "Write first, asking permission to submit your songs"!

Record sales throughout the world account for billions upon billions of dollars, with the United States accounting for at least half of this market. The others are the United Kingdom, Canada, and Japan.

Record companies are responsible for releasing the mechanical products of the music industry—records, cassettes, and CDs. These record companies not only control most of the biggest entertainers in the business today, but they also help select the songs these artists will record. There are record companies in every part of the world, and your song may become a hit in another country before receiving acceptance in the United States, so to give you an added chance for SELLING SONGS SUCCESSFULLY, I have listed companies in the United Kingdom and Canada.

You may note that I have left out some major record labels with which you are familiar. I have done this intentionally because, to give you that added jump on your competition, I have tried to list only those that my experience and research shows will be *open* and *receptive* to you, the new songwriter.

Don't eliminate any record company, especially the new and smaller ones listed here, because the smaller labels have come up with a fair share of hits and helped launch many a new artist and songwriter to success. These are also very often in need of artists and songs, making them *very* receptive to talented newcomers.

All these "RECORD COMPANIES AND RECORD PRODUCERS" accept all types of songs. This list is followed by a "SPECIAL" listing, mainly for country and western songwriters.

When you write to any record company or producer for permission, ask what type of songs they are looking for at that time, and whether to submit them by tape or cassette. I have tried to give you the *contact names* to reach so that they will be more receptive to you. Remember, a record is a *must,* so visit or write to as many of these record companies and record producers as possible.

For additional up-do-date listings of the many new faces that pop up on the record scene every day, pick up the important trade magazines such as *Billboard and Cashbox*. May GOOD FORTUNE smile on your songs and may your head and records spin with success!

RECORD COMPANIES
(USA)

Attack Records
Box 3161
Atlanta, GA 30302
Attn: C.E. Scott

AVC Records
6201 Sunset Blvd. (Suite 200)
Hollywood, CA 90028
Attn: James Warsinske

Black Diamond Records, Inc.
P.O. Box 8023
Pittsburg, CA 94565
Attn: Jerry "J"

Bolivia Records
1219 Kerlin Ave.
Brewton, AL 36426
Attn: Roy Edwards

Disc-Tinct Music, Inc.
111 Cedar Lane
Englewood, NJ 07631
Attn: Jeffrey Collins

Empty Sky Records
P.O. Box 626
Verplanck, NY 10596
Attn: Rick Carbone

EMZEE Records
Box 3213
S. Farmingdale, NY 11735
Attn: Dawn Kendall

Farr Records
Box 1098
Somerville, NJ 08876
Attn: Candace Campbell

Golden Triangle Records
1051 Saxonburg Blvd.
Glenshaw, PA 15116
Attn: Sunny James

Goldwax Record Co., Inc.
3181 Poplar Ave. (Suite 325)
Memphis, TN 38130
Attn: Jimmy Willis

Happy Man Records
Box 73, 4501 Spring Creek Dr.
Bonita Springs, FL 33923
Attn: Dick O'Britts

Master-Trak Enterprises
413 N. Parkerson
Crowley, LA 70526
Attn: Mark Miller

Miles Ahead Records
P.O. Box 34559
Los Angeles, CA 90035
Attn: Robert Riley

Missile Records
Box 5537, Kreole Station
Moss Point, MS 39563
Attn: Joe F. Mitchell

New Experience Records
Box 683
Lima, OH 45802
Attn: Tanya Milligan

Ocean Records, Inc.
P.O. Box 190944
Roxbury, MA 02119
Attn: Jackie Whitehead

On Top Records
3081 NW 24th St.
Miami, FL 33167
Attn: Chavela Frazier

P.I.R.A.T.E. Records
5381 Hollywood Blvd. (Suite 250)
Hollywood, CA 90028
Attn: Jefflyn Dangerfield

PDS Records
Box 412477
Kansas City, MO 64141
Attn: A&R Dept.

Penguin Records, Inc.
#2, Box 3031, SW 27th Ave.
Miami, FL 33133
Attn: Gregory J. Winters

Peter Pan Industries
88 St. Francis Street
Newark, NJ 07105
Attn: Marianne Eggleston

Saddlestone Records
264 "H" Street, Box 8110-21
Blaine, WA 98230
Attn: Candice James

Sahara Records
4475 Allisonville Rd. (8th Fl.)
Indianapolis, IN 46205

Studio B Records
P.O. Box 295
Atco, NJ 08004
Attn: Bob Thomas

Trend Records
P.O. Box 201
Smyrna, GA 30081
Attn: Tom Hodges

Tug Boat Records
2514 Build America Dr.
Hampton, VA 23666
Attn: Judith Guthro

Wingate Records
Box 10895
Pleasonton, CA 94588
Attn: P. Hanna

Write Key Records
3716 W. 87th Street

Chicago, IL 60652
Attn: Bert Swanson

Young Star Productions, Inc.
5501 N. Broadway
Chicago, IL 60640
Attn: Starling Young, Jr.

Zanzibar Records
2019 Noble Street
Pittsburgh, PA 15218
Attn: John C. Antimary

RECORD COMPANIES (CANADA AND ENGLAND)

Duke Street Records
121 Logan Ave.
Toronto, Ontario M4M 249 Canada
Attn: Andrew S. Hermant

E.S.R. Records
61 Burnthouse Lane
Exeter, Devon EX2 6AZ
United Kingdom
Attn: John Greenslade

Hickory Lane Records
P.O. Box 2275
Vancouver, British Columbia V6B 3W5 Canada
Attn: Chris Michaels

Le Matt Music Ltd.
c/o Stewart House, Hill Bottom Rd.
Highwycome, Buckinghamshire
HP12 4HJ England
Attn: Ron or Cathrine Lee

Leopard Music
23 Thrayle House, Stockwell Rd.
London SW99 OXU England
Attn: Errol Jones

Loading Bay Records
586 Bristol Rd., Selly Oak
Birmingham B29 6BQ England
Attn: Duncan Finlayson

Nephelin Records
404 St-Henri
Montreal, Quebec H3C 2P5 Canada
Attn: Mario Rubnikowich

Nettwerk Productions
1250 W. 6th Ave.
Vancouver, British Columbia V6H IA5 Canada
Attn: Simon Hussey

Nightflite Records, Inc.
4091 Pheasant Run
Mississanga, Ontario L5L 2C2 Canada
Attn: Joey Cee

Rhino Records Ltd.
The Chilterns, France Hill Dr.
Chamberley Surrey GUI5 3QA England
Attn: Bruce White

Roto-Noto Music
148 Erin Ave.
Hamilton, Ontario L8K 4W3 Canada
Attn: R. Cousins

Sunshine Records Ltd.
228 Selkirk Ave.

Winnipeg, Manitoba R2W 2L6 Canada
Attn: Ness Michaels

RECORD PRODUCERS

ACR Productions
P.O. Box 5236
Lubbock, TX 79417
Attn: Dwaine Thomas

Allen-Martin Productions, Inc.
9701 Taylorville Rd.
Louisville, KY 40299
Attn: Nick Stevens

Bell Records International
Box 725
Daytona Beach, FL 32115
Attn: LeRoy Pritchett

Continental Communications Corp.
P.O. Box 565
Tappan, NY 10983
Attn: Gene Schwartz

Creative Music Services
838 Fountain St.
Woodbridge, CT 06525
Attn: Craig Calistro

D.B. Productions
2417 Hibiscus Rd.
Ft. Myers, FL 33905
Attn: Dennis "D.B." Allen

Mike De Leon Productions
14146 Woodstream
San Antonio, TX 78231
Attn: Mike De Leon

Edward De Miles
4475 Allisonville Rd., 8th Fl.
Indianapolis, IN 46205
Attn: Edward De Miles

Joel Diamond Entertainment
5370 Vanalden Ave.
Tarzana, CA 91356
Attn: Scott Goodman

Dino M Production Co.
2367 208th St. #7
Torrance, CA 90501
Attn: Dino Maddalone

Duane Music, Inc.
382 Clarence Ave.
Sunnydale, CA 94086
Attn: Garrie Thompson

E P Productions
7455 Lorge Cr.
Huntington Beach, CA 92647
Attn: Billy Purcell

8th Street Music
204 E. 8th St.
Dixon, IL 61021
Attn: Rob McInnis

Festival Studios
3413 Florida Ave.

Kenner, LA 70065
Attn: Rick Naiser/Michael Borrello

The Fricon Entertainment Co., Inc.
1048 S. Ogden Dr.
Los Angeles, CA 90019
Attn: Publishing Dept.

Happy Days Music
Box 852
Beverly Hills, CA 90213
Attn: Jeremy McClain

Hobar Productions
27 Newton Pl.
Irvington, NJ 071 1 1
Attn: Randall Burney

Inspire Productions, Inc.
302 E. Pettigrew St., Suite 101
Durham, NC 27701
Attn: Willie Hill

Matthew Katz Productions
29903 Harvester Rd.
Malibu, CA 90265
Attn: Matthew Katz

Kingston Records and Talent
15 Exeter Rd.
Kingston, NH 03848
Attn: Harry Mann

Linear Cycle Productions
Box 2608
Sepulveda, CA 91393
Attn: R. Borowy

Chuck Mymit Music Productions
   9840 64th Ave.
   Flushing, NY 11374
   Attn: Chuck & Monte Mymit

Nashville Int'l. Entertainment Group
   Box 121076
   Nashville, TN 37212
   Attn: Reggie M. Churchwell

Pine Island Music
   9430 Live Oak Place
   Ft. Lauderdale, FL 33324
   Attn: Jack P. Bluestein

The Prescription Company
   70 Murray Ave.
   Port Washington, NY 10050
   Attn: David F. Gasman

Segal's Productions
   16 Grace Rd.
   Newton, MA 02159
   Attn: Charles Segal

Jack Stang
   753 Capitol Ave.
   Hartford, CT 06106
   Attn: Jack Stang

The Weisman Production Group
   449 N. Vista St.
   Los Angeles, CA 90036
   Attn: Ben Weisman

Frank Willson
   Box 2297

Universal City, TX 78148
Attn: Frank Willson

The Country and Western field merits a separate listing of record companies and record producers because of their unusual receptiveness, interest, and kindness to new songwriters everywhere. The heart of the C&W activity is in Nashville, with California and Texas also showing a lot of action. If you look at the C&W listings, you will note that most of the marketplaces are located in these areas, and more country and western hit songs come from these areas alone than from anywhere else. Obviously, this market warrants your utmost attention and effort, especially if your talent lies in the writing of C&W or folk-type songs, or even pop songs that can be geared for these buyers.

The following listing of record companies and record producers are known to be most receptive to you, the new, unknown songwriter, and you should try to reach each and every one of them. Tell them a little about yourself and ask how many songs to submit and whether they prefer tape or cassette. (Most will prefer cassette for easy handling and convenience.)

Alear Records
c/o McCoy, Route 2, Box 114
Berkeley Springs, WV 25411
Attn: Jim McCoy

AMI Records
394 W. Main St.
Hendersonville, TN 37075
Attn: Kevin Waugh

Bagatelle Record Company
400 San Jacinto St.
Houston, TX 77002
Attn: Byron Benton

Beau-Jim Records, Inc.
Box 2401
Sarasota, FL 34230
Attn: Buddy Hooper

Belmont Records
484 Lexington St.
Waltham, MA 02154
Attn: John Penny

BGM Records
8806 Lockway
San Antonio, TX 78217
Attn: Bill Green

Blue Gem Records
Box 29688
Hollywood, CA 90029
Attn: Pete Martin

Briarhill Records
3484 Nicolette Dr.
Crete, IL 60417
Attn: Danny Mack

BSW Records
P.O. Box 2297
Universal City, TX 78148
Attn: Frank Wilson

Bull City Records
Box 6
Rougemont, NC 27572
Attn: Freddie Roberts

Cedar Creek Records
44 Music Square E., Suite 503
Nashville, TN 37203
Attn: Larry Duncan

Cherry Records
9717 Jenson Dr.
Houston, TX 77093
Attn: A.V. Mittelstedt

Comstock Records Ltd.
10603 N. Hayden Rd., Suite 114
Scottsdale, AZ 85260
Attn: Patty Parker

Continental Records
744 Joppa Farm Rd.
Joppetowne, MD 21085
Attn: Ernest W. Cash

Country Breeze Records
1715 Marty
Kansas City, KS 66103
Attn: Ed Morgan

Country Star International
439 Wiley Ave.
Franklin, PA 16323
Attn: Norman Kelly

Crown Music Company
P.O. Box 2363
Brentwood, TN 37024
Attn: E. Burton

Eye Kill Records
Box 242
Woodland, PA 16881
Attn: John Wesley

Fountain Records
1203 Biltmore Ave.
High Point, NC 27260
Attn: Doris W. Lindsay

Fretboard Publishing
P.O. Box 40855
Nashville, TN 37204
Attn: A&R Dept.

Harmony Street Records
Box 4107
Kansas City, KS 66104
Attn: Charles Beth

Interstate 40 Records
900 19th Ave., S. Apt. 106
Nashville, TN 37212
Attn: Eddie Lee Carr

Jalyn Recording Company
306 Millwood Dr.
Nashville, TN 37217
Attn: Jack Lynch

Landmark Communications Group
Box 148296

Nashville, TN 37214
Attn: Bill Anderson, Jr.

Lari-jon Records
325 W. Walnut
Rising City, NE 68658
Attn: Larry Good

Lark Record Productions, Inc.
4815 S. Harvard, Suite 520
Tulsa, OK 74135
Attn: Sue Teaff

LRJ Record Co.
Box 3
Belen, NM 87002
Attn: Tony Palmer

The Mathes Company
P.O. Box 22653
Nashville, TN 37202
Attn: David Mathes

Mule Kick Records
5341 Silverlode Dr.
Placerville, CA 95667
Attn: Doug McGinnis, Sr.

Orbit Records
P.O. Box 120675
Nashville, TN 37212
Attn: Ray McGinnis

Pajer Records
23 Forest Lane
Black Mountain, NC 38711
Attn: Jerry Caldwell

Paragold Records
Box 292101
Nashville, TN 37229
Attn: Teresa Parks Bernard

Pilot Records and Tape Co.
628 S. South St.
Mount Airy, NC 27030
Attn: Paul E. Johnson

Playback Records
Box 630755
Miami, FL 33163
Attn: Jack Gale

Puzzle Records
Box 461892
Garland, TX 75046
Attn: Don Ferguson

San-Sue Recording Studio
Box 773
Mt. Juliet, TN 37122
Attn: Buddy Powell

Seaside Records
100 Labon St.
Tabor City, NC 28463
Attn: Elson H. Stevens

Sound Masters
9717 Jensen Dr.
Houston, TX 77093
Attn: A.V. Mittelstedt

Stardust Records
Box 13

Estill Springs, TN 37330
Attn: Buster Doss

Stark Records and Tape Co.
628 S. South St.
Mount Airy, NC 27030
Attn: Paul E. Johnson

Ten Squared, Inc.
P.O. Box 865
N. Hollywood, CA 91603
Attn: Michael Wenslow

Treasure Coast Records
692 SE Port St., Lucie Blvd.
Port St. Lucie, FL 34984
Attn: J.A. Blecha

Vokes Music Publ., & Record Co.
Box 12
New Kensington, PA 15068
Attn: Howard Vokes

Wence Sense Music
P.O. Box 110829
Nashville, TN 37222
Attn: Kathy Gaddes

Woodrich Records
Box 38
Lexington, AL 35648
Attn: Woody Richardson

Yellow Jacket Records
10303 Hickory Valley
Ft. Wayne, IN 46835
Attn: Allan Straten

Young Country Records
P.O. Box 5412
Buena Park, CA 90620
Attn: Leo J. Eiffert, Jr.

Zone Record Company
2674 Steele
Memphis, TN 38127
Attn: Marshall E. Ellis

C & W RECORD PRODUCERS

Alpha Music Productions
Box 14701
Lenexa, KS 66285
Attn: Glenn Major

Peter L. Bonta
2200 Airport Ave.
Fredericksburg, VA 22401
Attn: Buffalo Bob

Carolina Pride Productions
Box 6
Rougemont, NC 27572
Attn: Freddie Roberts

Eddie Carr
900 10th Ave., Apt. 106
Nashville, TN 37212
Attn: Eddie Carr

Country Reel Enterprises
P.O. Box 99307
Stockton, CA 95209
Attn: Mr. Dana C. Copenhaver

Country Star Productions
Box 569
Franklin, PA 16323
Attn: Norman Kelly

Col. Buster Doss Presents
Box 13
Estill Springs, TN 37330
Attn: Col. Buster Doss

Leo J. Eiffert, Jr.
Box 5412
Buena Park, CA 90620
Attn: Leo J. Eiffert, Jr.

Jack Gale
Box 630755
Miami, FL 33163
Attn: Jack Gale

Horizon Recording Studio
Rte. 1, Box 306
Seguin, TX 78155
Attn: H.M. Byron

Neal James Productions
P.O. Box 121626
Nashville, TN 37212
Attn: Neal James

Ralph D. Johnson
114 Catalpa Dr.
Mt. Juliet, TN 37122
Attn: Ralph D. Johnson

Gene Kennedy Enterprises, Inc.
3950 N. Mt. Juliet Rd.

Mt. Juliet, TN 37122
Attn: Gene Kennedy

Frank E. Koehl
6223 N. 51st Ave.
Glendale, AZ 85301
Attn: Frank E. Koehl

Landmark Audio of Nashville
Box 148296
Nashville, TN 37214
Attn: Bill Anderson, Jr.

Lark Record Productions
Box 35726
Tulsa, OK 74153
Attn: Jana Jac

Lemon Square Productions
P.O. Box 671008
Dallas, TX 75367
Attn: Mike Anthony

Jim McCoy Productions
Rt. 2, Box 114
Berkeley Springs, WV 25411
Attn: Jim McCoy

Pete Martin Productions
Box 29688
Hollywood, CA 90029
Attn: Pete Martin

David Mathes Productions
P.O. Box 22653
Nashville, TN 37202
Attn: David W. Mathes

Midwest Records
3611 Cleveland Ave.
Lincoln, NE 68504
Attn: Harold Dennis

Nebro Record Company
Box 194
New Hope, AL 35760
Attn: Reggie M. Churchwell

Bill Nelson
45 Perham St., W.
Roxbury, MA 02131
Attn: Bill Nelson

Patty Parker
10603 N. Hayden Rd., Suite 114
Scottsdale, AZ 85260
Attn: Patty Parker

Jim Pierce
101 Hurts Ln.
Hendersonville, TN 37075
Attn: Jim Pierce

TMC Productions
P.O. Box 12353
San Antonio, TX 78212
Attn: Joe Scates

Trac Record Company
170 N. Maple
Fresno, CA 93702
Attn: Stan Anderson

Wilbur Productions
159 W. 4th St., #10

New York, NY 10014
Attn: Will Schillinger

Frank Willson
Box 2297
Universal City, TX 78148
Attn: Frank Willson

Wright Productions
11231 Hwy. 64 E.
Tyler, TX 75707
Attn: Record Producer

Music publishers take over the hard business realities of selling songs by handling the contact end of getting your gong recorded, copyrighting, collecting royalties, contract negotiations, and promotion. They handle all these functions and more that must be taken care of expertly if you are to be a creative, financial success.

They enable you to concentrate on the creative aspects of your talent and leave the music industry know-how to them. Music publishers also know which artists, record companies, producers, and other important contacts are currently in the market for new songs.

These music publishers accept all types of songs but look for "crossover" potential in them. Crossover means that your song can go from pop to C&W to R&B, if appropriate, thus adding to your song's appeal and increasing its revenue-generating potential.

As with the record companies listed previously, I am adding Music Publishers in Canada and the United Kingdom, since they have easier access to the international market and you may find an easier route to your SELLING SONGS SUCCESSFULLY through them.

Following these Music Publishers, whom I know to accept all types of songs, I have listed the most receptive country and western music publishers for those of you who feel your songs fit into this category. Remember—these C&W music publishers are the kindest, most attentive, and most helpful people to the new songwriter in the music business today.

MUSIC PUBLISHERS

Alexis Publishers
Box 532
Malibu, CA 90265
Attn: Lee Magid

Amalgamated Tulip Corp
117 W. Rockland Rd. Box 615
Libertyville, IL 60048
Attn: Perry Johnson

Apon Publishing Co.
Box 3082, Steinway Station
Long Island City, NY 11103
Attn: Don Zeiman

Bad Grammar Music
825 Sierra Vista, Suite 320
Las Vegas, NV 89109
Attn: Joe Trupiano

Bal & Bal Music Publishing Co.
P.O. Box 369
LaCanada, CA 91012
Attn: Adrian P. Bal

Earl Beecher Publishing
P.O. Box 21 11

Huntington Beach, CA 92647
Attn: Earl Beecher

Best Buddies, Inc.
2100 8th Ave., S.
Nashville, TN 37204
Attn: Review Committee

Beth-Ridge Music Publ., Co.
1508 Harlem, Suite 204
Memphis, TN 38114
Attn: Janelle Rachall

Bok Music
P.O. Box 17838
Encino, CA 91416
Attn: Monica Benson

C.A.B. Independent Publ., Co.
P.O. Box 26852
Oklahoma City, OK 73126
Attn: Christopher Stanley

California Country Music
112 Widmar Pl.
Clayton, CA 94517
Attn: Edgar J. Brincat

Ernie Cash Music, Inc.
744 Joppa Farm Rd.
Joppa, MD 21085
Attn: Ernest W. Cash

Cheavoria Music Co.
1219 Kerlin Ave.
Brewton, AL 36426
Attn: Roy Edwards

Clientele Music
  252 Bayshore Dr.
  Hendersonville, TN 37075
  Attn: Thornton Cline

Coffee & Cream Publ., Co.
  1138 E. Price St.
  Philadelphia, PA 19138
  Attn: Bolden Abrams, Jr.

Cosgroove Music, Inc.
  Box 2234
  Amagansett, NY 11930
  Attn: Lance Cosgrove

Cude & Pickens Publishing
  5 1 9 N. Halifax Ave.
  Dayton, FL 32118
  Attn: Bobby Lee Cude

Dore Records
  1608 Argyle
  Hollywood, CA 90028
  Attn: Lew Bedell

Dream Sequence Music, Ltd.
  P.O. Box 2194
  Charlottesville, VA 22902
  Attn: Kevin McNoidy

Earthscream Music Publ., Co.
  8377 Westview Dr.
  Houston, TX 77055
  Attn: Jeff Johnson

Emperor of Emporers
  16133 Fairview Ave.

Fontana, CA 92336
Attn: Stephen V. Mann

Empty Sky Music Co.
14th St., P.O. Box 626
Verplanck, NY 10596
Attn: Lisa Lancaster

EMZEE Music
Box 3213
S. Farmingdale, NY 11735
Attn: Maryann Zalesak

Excursion Musici Group
P.O. Box 9248
San Jose, CA 95157
Attn: Frank T. Prins

Famous Music Publ., Companies
3500 W. Olive Ave., Suite 1000
Burbank, CA 91505
Attn: Creative Dept.

First Release Music Publ.
6124 Selma Ave.
Hollywood, CA 90028
Attn: Danny Howell

Four Newton Publ.
Rt.1, Box 187-A
Whitney, TX 76692
Attn: Allen Newton

Frick Music Publ., Co.
404 Bluegrass Ave.
Madison, TN 37115
Attn: Bob Frick

Frog and Moose Music
Box 40784
Nashville, TN 37204
Attn: Steven R. Pinkston

Alan Gary Music
P.O. Box 179
Palisades Park, NJ 07650
Attn: Alan Gary

Giftness Enterprises
1315 Simpson Rd., NW, Suite #5
Atlanta, GA 30314
Attn: New Song Dept.

Go Star Music
4700 Belle Grove Rd., Suite #20
Baltimore, MD 21225
Attn: William E. Baker

Jay Gold Music Publ.
P.O. Box 409
East Meadow, NY 11554
Attn: Jay Gold

Richard E. Gowell Music
45 7th St.
Auburn, ME 04210
Attn: Rich Gowell

Green Meadows Publ.
Rt. #4, Box 92, Charlotte Dr.
Beaver Dam, KY 42320
Attn: Robert Bailey

Hamstein Publ., Co., Inc.
P.O. Box 163870

Austin, TX 78716
Attn: Director, Creative Services

Harmony Street Music
Box 4107
Kansas City, KS 66104
Attn: Charles Beth

Heaven Songs
16776 Lakeshore Dr., C-300
Lake Elsinore, CA 92330
Attn: Dave Paton

High Desert Music Co.
29526 Peoria Rd.
Halsey, OR 97348
Attn: Karl V. Black

Hitsource Publishing
1324 Oakton
Evanston, IL 60602
Attn: Alan J. Goldberg

Jedo Inc.
5062 Calatrana Dr.
Los Angeles, CA 91364
Attn: Jon Divirian

Jof-Dave Music
1055 Kimball Ave.
Kansas City, KS 66104
Attn: David E. Johnson

Jungle Boy Music
1230 Hill St.
Santa Monica, CA 90405
Attn: Robert Anderson

Just A Note Music
1058 E. Saint Catherine
Louisville, KY 40204
Attn: John V. Heath

Kaupps & Robert Publ., Co.
P.O. Box 5474
Stockton, CA 95205
Attn: Nancy L. Marrihew

Koke, Moke & Noke Music
Box 724677
Atlanta, GA 30339
Attn: Bryan Cole

Kommunication Koncepts
Box 2095
Philadelphia, PA 19103
Attn: S. Deane Henderson

Le Grande Fromage
8739 Sunset Blvd.
Los Angeles, CA 90069
Attn: Jan Rhees

Lighthouse Music Co., Inc.
2 Cielo Ctr., 1250 Loop 360 S.
Austin, TX 78746
Attn: Bitsy Rice

Lineage Publishing Co.
Box 211
East Prairie, MO 63845
Attn: Tommy Loomas

Little Pond Productions
P.O. Box 20594

Portland, OR 97220
Attn: JoAnna Burns-Miller

Loveforce International
P.O. Box 241648
Los Angeles, CA 90024
Attn: T. Wilkins

Andy Marvel Music
P.O. Box 133
Farmingdale, NY 11738
Attn: Andy Marvel

Media Productions
1001 1/2 Elizabeth St.
Oak Hill, WV 25901
Attn: Doug Gent

Miracle Mile Music
P.O. Box 35449
Los Angeles, CA 90035
Attn: Robert Riley

Music Sales Corporation
225 Park Ave., S.
New York, NY 10003
Attn: Philip "Flip" Black

The Joseph Nicoletd Music Co.
P.O. Box 2818
Newport Beach, CA 92659
Attn: Joseph Nicoletti

Non-Stop Music Publishing
915 W. 100 South
Salt Lake City, UT 84104
Attn: Michael L. Dowdle

Ohisher Music
   P.O. Box 202814
   Oklahoma City, OK 73156
   Attn: Mickey Sherman

One Hot Note Music Inc.
   P.O. Box 454 Main St.
   Cold Springs Harbor, NY 11724
   Attn: Greg MacMillan

Peermusic
   8159 Hollywood Blvd.
   Los Angeles, CA 90069
   Attn: Nicole Mahuchet

RECORD COMPANIES
(CANADA AND ENGLAND)

Alleged Iguana Music
   44 Archdekin Dr.
   Brampton, Ontario L6V IY4 Canada
   Attn: Randall Cousins

Berandol Music Ltd.
   2600 John St., Unit 220
   Markham, Ontario L3R 3W3 Canada
   Attn: Ralph Cruikshank

Blenheim Music
   14 Brickendon Green
   Hertford S91 38PB England
   Attn: John Dye

Cod Oil Productions Ltd.
   Box 8568, St. John's
   Newfoundland AIB 3P2 Canada
   Attn: Wilson Temple

Creole Music Ltd.
   The Chilterns, France Hill Dr.
   Camberley, Surrey GUI5 3QA England
   Attn: Bruce White

F & J Music
   23 Thrayle House, Stockwell Rd.
   London SW9 OXU England
   Attn: Errol Jones

First Time Music Publ., Ltd.
   Sovereign House, 12 Trewartha Rd., Praa Sands
   Penzance, Cornwall TR20 8ST England
   Attn: Roderick G. Jones

Graduate Music Ltd.
   St. Swithun's Institute, The Trinity
   Worcester WRI 2PN England
   Attn: David Virr

Keep Calm Music Ltd.
   Falcon Mews
   London SWI2 9SJ England
   Attn: Joanna Underwood

Montana Music
   Box 702, Snowdon Station
   Montreal, Quebec H3X 3X8 Canada
   Attn: David P. Leonard

Nervous Publishing
   4/36 Dabbs Hill Lane, Northolt
   Middle Sex, London, England
   Attn: Roy Williams

R.T.L. Music
   c/o Stewart House, Hillbottom Rd.

Highwycome, Buckinghamshire, England
Attn: Ron Lee

William Seip Music Incorporated
Box 515
Waterloo, Ontario N2J 4A9 Canada
Attn: William Seip

Sphenmusations
12 Northfield Rd., Onehouse,
Stowmarket Suffolk 1PI4 3HR England
Attn: James Butt

C & W MUSIC PUBLISHERS

Aim High Music Company
1300 Division St.
Nashville, TN 37203
Attn: Metzgar

Allisongs Inc.
1603 Horton Ave.
Nashville, TN 37212
Attn: Jim Allison

Axbar Productions
Box 12353
San Antonio, TX 78212
Attn: Joe Scates

Better Times Publishing
1203 Biltmore Ave.
High Point, NC 27260
Attn: Doris Lindsay

Betty Jane/Josie Jane Music Publ.
7400 N. Adams Rd.

North Adams, MI 49262
Attn: Claude E. Ree

Blue Hill Music
308 Munger Lane
Bethlehem, CT 06751
Attn: Paul Hotchkiss

BoDe Music
18016 S. Western Ave., Suite 228
Gardena, CA 90248
Attn: Tory Gullett

Bill Butler Music
P.O. Box 20
Hondo, TX 78861
Attn: Bill Butler

Calinoh Music Group
1208 16th Ave., S., Suite #8
Nashville, TN 37212
Attn: Ann Hofer or Tom Cornett

Castle Music Corp.
50 Music Square W., Suite 201
Nashville, TN 37203
Attn: Eddie Russell

Cedar Creek Music
44 Music Square E., Suite 503
Nashville, TN 37203
Attn: Larry Duncan

Sonny Christopher Publishing
P.O. Box 9144
Ft. Worth, TX 76147
Attn: Sonny Christopher

Jerry Connell Publishing, Co.
130 Pilgrim Dr.
San Antonio, TX 78213
Attn: Jerry Connell

The Cornelius Companies
1017 17th Ave., S., Suite 1
Nashville, TN 37212
Attn: Ron Cornelius

Country Breeze Music
1715 Marty
Kansas City, KS 66103
Attn: Ed Morgan

Country Star Music
439 Wiley Ave.
Franklin, PA 16323
Attn: Norman Kelly

Loman Craig Music
P.O. Box 111480
Nashville, TN 37222
Attn: Loman Craig

Creekside Music
100 Labon St.
Tabor City, NC 28463
Attn: Elson H. Stevens

Cupit Music
P.O. Box 121904
Nashville, TN 37212
Attn: Jerry Cupit

Dan The Man Music
19465 Lorain Rd., Suite 12

Cleveland, OH 44126
Attn: Daniel L. Bischoff

Darbonne Publishing, Co.
Route 3, Box 172
Haynesville, IA 71038
Attn: Edward N. Dettenheim

Denny Music Group
3325 Fairmont Dr.
Nashville, TN 37203
Attn: Pandora Denny

Diamond Wind Music
P.O. Box 311
Estero, FL 33298
Attn: Reenie Diamond

Doc Publishing
2514 Build America Dr.
Hampton, VA 23666
Attn: Judith Guthrie

Entertainment Services Music Group
42 Music Square W.
Nashville, TN 37203
Attn: Curt Conroy

Doug Faiella Publishing
16591 County Home Rd.
Marysville, OH 43040
Attn: Doug Faiella

Five Roses Music Group
P.O. Box 417
White Sulphur Springs, NY 12787
Attn: Sammy Lee Marler

Henderson Group Music
125 Powell Mill Rd.
Spartanburg, SC 2!9301
Attn: Dr. Barry Henderson

Hitsburgh Music Company
P.O. Box 1431, 233 N. Electra
Gallatin, TN 37066
Attn: Harold Gilbert

Iron Skillet Music
B-105, Richard Jones Rd.
Nashville, TN 37215
Attn: Claude G. Southall

Jellee Works Music
P.O. Box 16572
Kansas City, MO 64133
Attn: Jimmy Lee

Little Richie Johnson Music
318 Horizon Vista Blvd.
Helen, NM 87002
Attn: Tony Palmer

Al Jolson Black & White Music
114 175th Ave., S.
Nashville, TN 37203
Attn: Albert Jolson

Kansas Records Corp.
P.O. Box 1014
Lebanon, TN 37088
Attn: Kit Johnson

Karen Kaylee Music Group
R.O. #11, Box 360

Greensburg, PA 15601
Attn: Karen Kaylee

Gene Kennedy Enterprises, Inc.
3950 N. Mt. Juliet Rd.
Mt. Juliet, TN 37122
Attn: Gene Kennedy

Lion Hill Music Publ., Co.
P.O. Box 110983
Nashville, TN 37222
Attn: Wayne G. Loinsz

The Lithics Group
P.O. Box 272
Garden City, AL 35070
Attn: Dennis N. Kahler

Lovey Music, Inc.
P.O. Box 360755
Miami, FL 33163
Attn: Jack Gale

The Lowery Group
3051 Clairmont Rd., NE
Atlanta, GA 30329
Attn: Cotton Carrier

The Marco Music Group, Inc.
P.O. Box 24454
Nashville, TN 37202
Attn: Jeff Hollandsworth

Merry Marilyn Music Publ.
33717 View Crest Dr.
Lake Elsinore, CA 92532
Attn: Marilyn Hendricks

Music in the Right Keys Publ., Co.
3716 W. 8th St.
Chicago, IL 60652
Attn: Bert Swanson

Old Slowpoke Music
P.O. Box 52681
Tulsa, OK 74152
Attn: Rodney Young

Pecos Valley Music
2709 West Pine Lodge
Roswell, NM 88201
Attn: Ray Wilmon

Justin Peters Music
3609 Donna Kay Dr.
Nashville, TN 37211
Attn: Justin Peters

Jimmy Price Music Publ.
1662 Wyatt Parkway
Lexington, KY 40505
Attn: Jimmy Price

Red Boots Tunes
5503 Roosevelt Way NE
Seattle, WA 98105
Attn: Music Publisher

Steve Rose Music
115 E. 34th St., #6K
New York, NY 10016
Attn: Steve Rose

Samuel Three Productions
4056 Shady Valley Dr.

Arlington, TX 76103
Attn: Samuel Egnot

Sellwood Publishing
170 N. Maple
Fresno, CA 93702
Attn: Stan Anderson

Silver Thunder Music Group
P.O. Box 41335
Nashville, TN 37204
Attn: Rusty Budde

Sound Column Publications
Country Manor, 812 S. 890 E.
Orem, UT 84058
Attn: Ron Simpson

Starbound Publ., Co.
207 Winding Rd.
Friendswood, TX 77546
Attn: Buz Hart

Tek Publishing
P.O. Box 1485
Lake Charles, LA 70602
Attn: Eddie Shuler

Tiki Enterprises, Inc.
195 S. 26th St.
San Jose, CA 95116
Attn: Gradie O'Neal

Tompaul Music Company
628 South St.

Mount Airy, NC 27030
Attn: Paul E. Johnson

Two Fold Music
P.O. Box 388
Goodlettsville, TN 37072
Attn: Roland Pope

Shane Wilder Music
P.O. Box 3503
Hollywood, CA 90078
Attn: Shane Wilder

Wind Haven Publishing
6477 Emerson Ave., S.
St. Petersburg, FL 33707
Attn: Joe Terry

Woodrich Publishing Co.
P.O. Box 38
Lexington, AL 35648
Attn: Woody Richardson

In some cases, many aspiring songwriters write songs with a particular artist in mind they would like to reach to possibly record it! For these songwriters, I am including a listing of major recording labels for whom they record.

Always address the artist in care of their record label! If you'd also like to take a stab at the record company alone, simply address your letter or package, ATTN: A&R Department in care of the record label. In both cases, *always enclose an SASE* for their convenience and reply. Lots of good luck here!!

MAJOR RECORD COMPANIES

A & M Records
595 Madison Ave.
New York, NY 10022

Arista Records
6 West 57th St.
New York, NY 10019

Atco (Atlantic)
75 Rockefeller Plaza
New York, NY 10019

B M G Records
1133 Avenue of the Americas
New York NY 10036

Capitol Records
1750 N. Vine St.
Hollywood, CA 90028

CBS/Sony Records, Inc.
51 West 52nd St.
New York, NY 10019

Columbia Records/Epic
P.O. Box 4450
New York NY 10101

Criterian Music Corp.
6124 Selma Ave.
Hollywood, CA 90028

Curb Records
3907 W. Alameda Ave.
Burbank, CA 91505

Cypress Records
1525 Crossroads of the World
Los Angeles, CA 90028

DEF American
c/o Rick Rubin
3500 W. Olive Ave.
Burbank, CA 91505

DGC Records
9130 Sunset Blvd.
Los Angeles, CA 90069

Elektra Entertainment
75 Rockefeller Plaza
New York, NY 10019

EMI Records
810 Seventh Ave.
New York, NY 10019

Geffen Records
9126 Sunset Blvd.
Los Angeles, CA 90069

Island Records
14 East 4th St.
New York, NY 10012

Leface Records
3500 Parkway Lane
Atlanta, GA 30092

London Records/Polydor
825 Eighth Ave.
New York, NY 10019

MCA Records
70 Universal City Plaza
Universal City, CA 91608

Mercury Records/Polygram
825 Eighth Ave.
New York, NY 10019

Motown Records
6255 Sunset Blvd.
Los Angeles, CA 90028

Philadelphia International Records
309 S. Broad St.
Philadelphia, PA 19107

RCA Records
1133 Avenue of the Americas
New York, NY 10036

Reprise Records/Warner Bros.
3300 Warner Blvd.
Burbank, CA 91505

Rhino Records
2225 Colorado Ave.
Santa Monica, CA 90404

SBK Records
1290 Avenue of the Americas
New York, NY 10014

Scotti Bros.
2114 Pico Blvd.
Santa Monica, CA 90405

WEA Records
111 N. Hollywood Way
Burbank, CA 91505

Zomba Recording Corp.
137-139 West 25th St.
New York, NY 10001

INDEX

A
A&R   34, 46, 51–57, 61, 97, 125, 136, 163
Airplay   10, 75, 78, 71
American Society of Composers, Authors and Publishers   See ASCAP
Angles and deals   113–114
Artists   1, 2, 10, 19, 25–26, 38, 46, 49, 51, 53–58, 61–62, 70–72, 77, 97, 100, 103, 118, 120, 144
Artists and Repertoire men   See A&R
ASCAP   82–86, 89

B
Billboard   10, 38, 96, 123
BMI   82, 86–91, 95

C
C&W   50, 67, 94–98, 103, 133, 144–145
  market   98
  songs   94, 103
Carmichael, Hoagy   65
Cashbox   10, 123
Church   50, 102, 132, 143
Clearance Societies   81–82
Collaborators   66
Contacts   49–50
Copyright law   82–84, 91, 107
Copyright Office   106–108
Copyrighting   105, 144
Cost   25, 46, 68, 71–72, 83–85, 90–91, 107
Country and western   46, 76, 93–94, 118, 122, 133, 145   See also C&W
Creative hustle   9–10, 45
Crewe, Bob   57
Criticism   69–70
Cry   50

D
Decca Records   100
Demonstration records   See demos

Demos   2, 24–25, 46, 59, 68, 119–120
Disc jockey   1, 10, 31, 75–77

E
Echo   67, 76
Emotions   55, 67, 76, 94
Entertainers   11, 50, 61, 122
Enthusiasm   5–7

F
Fifth Dimension   103
Four Seasons   57

G
Genius Incorporated   57
Glazer, Tom   67
Gordy, Berry, Jr.   17–18, 66

H
Hair   102–103
Hammerstein   See Rodgers and Hammerstein
Hart   See Rodgers and Hart
Herbert, Victor   66
Hustle   9–11, 13–15, 17, 23, 45, 78, 119
  See also creative hustle, physical hustle

I
Indie Record Producers   55, 57, 120
Initiative   13–14, 70

L
Lead-sheet   23–25, 53, 59, 68, 97, 106–107, 117–118
Lerner and Loewe   65
Letters   30, 38–39, 77, 120
Local boy image   76
Loewe   See Lerner and Loewe
Lyric   6, 19, 24–25, 53, 66–68, 70, 83–84, 94–96, 100–102, 109–110, 118

M

Mailing 45–47, 68, 71, 120
Marketplaces 98, 121, 133
Master recording 56, 71
Miller, Roger 96, 101, 124, 151
Miracles, The 17–18
Motown 18, 66, 166
Music arranger 24
    director 76
    publishers 1, 25, 38–39, 57, 73, 83, 93, 97–98, 103–104, 144–145, 155
    Musical stage show 99–104
Musical stenographer 24
My Fair Lady 65, 100–101

N

Newspapers 29–31, 61, 68, 70, 96

O

Off-Broadway 102–103
Oldham, Andy 58
Oliver 103
One Life, One Love, One You 27, 42
Original cast 103

P

Performance royalties 78, 81, 87–89, 99
Physical hustle 9, 11
Postal card 42–43, 77
Preparing your song 23–26
Promotion 49, 71, 73–75, 77–79, 81, 144
Publicity 29–31, 38, 49, 74, 76

R

Radio station 31, 75–78, 81, 86
Ray, Johnny 50
RCA Victor 58
Record companies 56–57, 122
Recording 1–2, 20, 24–26, 30–31, 46, 49, 53–59, 62, 67–69, 71–75, 93, 95, 97, 100, 103, 106–107, 110, 114, 117–118, 120–121
Rejection 76, 116, 120
Repeat After Me 67
Return postage 53, 98, 120
Robinson, Smokey 18
Rodgers and Hammerstein 65
Rodgers and Hart 66
Rolling Stones, The 58

S

Selling points 37–39
Sherry 57
Singers 10, 19
Song title 25, 94, 96, 108–109
Song-plugger 74–75
Song-selling 111, 114, 119
Song sharks 109–111
Songwriters 1–2, 19–24, 29, 34, 37–39, 41, 58, 66–69, 71, 73–74, 81–82, 93–97, 100–104, 109–110, 113, 115, 120, 122, 133, 163
Songwriting 3, 6–7, 14, 20, 23–25, 30–31, 39, 66, 68, 74, 76–78, 109, 116
Stardust 65
Stick-to-itiveness 13–14
Stryker, Fred 67
Stuart, Marty 67
Success stories 12, 20

T

Teen magazine 62
Television 82, 85–87, 90, 96
Title 19, 25, 29, 42, 53, 66, 78, 82, 88, 94–97, 103, 107–109, 120
Trade magazine 10, 61, 74, 123
Tryout 102

V

Variety 10, 61

W

Way Over There 17
West Side Story 101